Proverbs 3:56

Julie ~
God loves you for now and
for always ~

My love ~
Maggie

Mommy, Where Were You?

By Migsie Jensen

Illustrated by Laura Bostrom

For I resolved to know nothing while I was with you except Jesus Christ and him crucified. I came to you in weakness and fear, and with much trembling. My message and my preaching were not with wise and persuasive words, but with a demonstration of the Spirit's power, so that your faith might not rest on men's wisdom, but on God's power.

(1 Corinthians 2:2–5 NIV)

In loving memory and honor of
my mother
who planted seeds of
faith
when I wasn't looking...

And dedicated to

Vern, My dear husband, who has been Jesus to me with skin on.

My Children
Cuf, who was born smiling and continues to reflect God's love as he gives that gift to everyone he meets.

Heather, who expresses God's love through the sacrificial giving of herself to all her life touches.

David, who has God's hand on his life I expect because he has the heart of David in his deep love for his Lord and Savior.

Steve, who has God's call on his life that has been molded and shaped by the challenges in his life to become a mighty witness for his Lord.

My Beautiful Stepdaughters
Julie, Becky, and Lori who have embraced me with their love.

To the wonderful sons and daughters that God has so graciously brought into my life through marriage…

…and all of our beautiful grandchildren

And most of all to My Wonderful Lord and Savior who was willing to use this broken vessel to carry His message of Love to His hurting children.

Special Thanks

To my husband Vern, who has been a constant source of patience and love, encouraging me to take a risk and step out of my comfort zone. His wisdom and good judgment have been instrumental in molding this manuscript into something worth reading.

To Greg Surratt, our senior pastor, who was willing to take a risk with two broken people to open the door to healing, restoration and changed lives and who allowed us to sit "on the bus"—a bus that hasn't stopped moving.

To Julie Hiott, who shared my passion for hurting women and came alongside as a partner and encourager for "The Mommy Group."

To Jennifer, Bonnie, Debbie, and **Penny**, who want so much to see healing in the lives of others that they were willing to be vulnerable enough to share the brokenness and heartaches of their own lives.

To Tami Cardnella, who after working in prison ministry insisted I had to tell it all.

To Sheena Martin, who has prayed me through this, lifting me up in times of frustration and discouragement—and there were many.

To Laura Bostrom, who gave me the shove I needed to pursue publication and whose love and sensitivity to God's heart shine through her artwork in these pages.

To Cathy Mart, whose passion for God flows through her music and who allowed that God-given gift to flow into the hearts of women through an audio recording available with this book.

To all my dear friends, who, after reading the manuscript, encouraged me to persevere in getting this book published.

To my Lord and Savior, who was my inspiration and my guide in this journey of faith.

CONTENTS

Introduction

There was a moment in time when I felt God placed a call on my life. With that came a passion for bringing healing to hurting women—women who have brokenness in their lives as a result of feeling neglected, rejected, or abandoned by their mothers.

That was the beginning of a journey on which God has taken me, a journey of discovery of healing, not only for them, but for myself as well. It was at that point that I felt God prompted me to start a group for these women that He called "Where Were You, Mommy?" Just an announcement of "that name" brought over twenty women to that first group.

I had never led a group without some kind of written format, but I felt that God wanted to lead it, through me, step by step, moment by moment. It wasn't an easy thing for me to wait on Him to reveal to me what He wanted to do, but He was faithful, and week by week He set the agenda.

I believed that He wanted to begin at the beginning of their lives, at the moment of conception. But at that first meeting when we were spending time getting acquainted, there was so much "chit chat" going on, I didn't know how to get us to the place where we could move deeper.

It was after that meeting when I felt He told me, "Wash their feet." Wash their feet? "Yes, wash their feet." So with the help of a dear friend who shared my passion, we brought pitchers, buckets, and towels. One by one, we washed the feet of these women.

Tears began to flow. The women who hardly knew one another began praying for each other and the walls that divided came tumbling down.

The following week we were ready to go to that place, the beginning place when and where their lives began. The Lord revealed Himself and brought healing to those secret places.

Week after week, He brought new revelations to me and to these women. Week by week, as the women gained a different perspective and a greater understanding of their mothers, their hearts began to soften. This made a way for them to come to a time and place where they were ready to forgive their moms and in so doing found release and relief in their lives and a sense of freedom and healing they had never known before. Not all of them had the same experience, but I believe all of them felt the touch of God in their lives in some way that was meaningful to them.

I learned a lot through the leading of that group, but I came to discover, too, that there was much more for me to learn. That was only the beginning. I had prayed for the healing of these women only to discover there was a lot of healing that still needed to take place in my own life. Healing seems to peel off in layers, and I still had a lot of layers. But God has continued to heal the memories and traumatic experiences of my life that in many ways had crippled me and kept me from becoming all He created me to be. I know He wants that for you as well.

It isn't easy to share what is in this book. I am laying open my life for all to see only because I believe it is what He wants me to do so that others will receive the healing that only He can give. As I was praying about it, I asked Him,

"Do you really want me to go naked before the whole world?"

His reply was, "That's what I did. Are you willing?"

I had to say "yes."

CHAPTER ONE
Where Were You, Mommy?

Where Were You, Mommy? Where were you, Mommy, when I needed you? My heart was crying out, "Mommy, where are you?"

It was dark in my room at night. Shadows would move across the walls. I know now it was only shadows caused by the moonlight peeking through my window. But Mommy, there were such strange shapes on my walls, sometimes moving, perhaps just a tree blowing in the wind—but I was so small, and they looked so big.

I didn't understand, and you weren't there to tell me it was only the moonlight shining through the trees. You weren't there to put your arms around me when I cried out. You weren't there to say, "It's okay, you are safe."

I wasn't very pretty as a little girl. I didn't run fast. I didn't talk a lot. I didn't laugh a lot. I didn't know how to make a friend or to be a friend. No one in the neighborhood picked me to be on their team as they played ball in the vacant lot next door. I can remember standing on the sidelines, watching all the others laugh and shout. I didn't know whether to stay or to run home. If I ran, they would make fun of me; if I stayed, they would ignore me. I wanted so much to run home to my mommy, to have you hold me and reassure me, but where were you, Mommy?

Sometimes there would be someone who would take me by the hand and say, "Come play with me. Come over to my house." But it was usually when they had no one else to play with. I would walk into their house. It felt so warm, so happy, and I could smell cookies in the oven. I saw a mom there ready and eager to welcome her daughter and her friend.

Then I would go home. It was dark in the house. You either weren't there or you were asleep, passed out from drinking or too depressed to face the day. The house didn't smell like fresh baked cookies. It smelled like dirty dishes left in the sink from the day before, or maybe days before. How I longed to have that warm, bright home to come home to and a mom to say, "Hi honey, how are you doing? How would some cookies and hot chocolate taste to you? Who is your little friend? How nice it is to have you here with us." But instead, I never wanted to bring my friends home. The house didn't smell nice, it wasn't very neat and clean, and there was no one there.

Where were you, Mommy?

I would walk to school, by myself or sometimes with a friend. I didn't know it was going to rain when I left for school, but oh, it rained so hard. I watched as all the other mothers would come to school and pick up their children. I would walk home in the rain. I got so wet, so cold.

Where were you, Mommy?

We were supposed to come home for lunch. I came home, but no one was there to fix me lunch. I opened a can of beans. Sometimes I ate them cold, right out of the can. I ate a lot of beans.

As I walked home from school, sometimes I would get teased or threatened by boys. They would twist my arm or make ugly comments. I guess they thought they were being funny, but I was frightened. I wanted to run as fast as I could—home to some loving, reassuring arms.

Where were you, Mommy?

I tried to tell you, but you wouldn't listen, you wouldn't believe me. He was touching me in places that didn't feel right. That frightened me. He was telling me to do things I didn't want to do, but I was afraid not to. I didn't understand what was going on. He was so much bigger than me, and he told me not to tell. It took all my courage to tell you, Mommy, but you didn't believe me! Mommy, I was so frightened and so alone. Why didn't you believe me? Why didn't you help me?

My body was starting to change. It felt different. I know I started to cry a lot. My feelings were hurt so easily. What was going on? I needed you to tell me about girl things. I needed you to show me what to do, to shop for those things that I needed that were so personal—so "mother and daughter"-y.

I was growing into womanhood and didn't even know it. Boys started to notice me as my breasts developed. I felt embarrassed, and I wanted to talk to you about what to do, what to say, how to act. After a while it started to feel good to me to have someone notice me. Before long the noticing moved to touching. It felt so good to be held by someone. It felt like love, but I didn't understand those feelings either. I wanted to talk to you about all that, but where were you?

There was one boy I liked a lot, and he asked me to a school dance. I was so excited about that! I wanted so much to look pretty, to have a new dress to wear, to have my hair fixed in a special way, to be fussed over by you. I wanted to share my excitement with you. I wanted you to tell me what to do, to give me guidance, but you weren't there.

As the years went by, so did my childhood. I feel like the little girl in me never came out to play. I had to do a lot of things around the house that mommies are supposed to do. I would have to take care of my little brother because you weren't there to do it. I loved my little brother, but I wasn't his mother—you were! I tried to clean the house. I tried to cook some things. I tried to wash clothes. I tried to take care of Daddy, too, but it wasn't my responsibility. I was still a little girl needing a mommy.

I didn't know how to do things well because no one was there to teach me. I did the best I could, but I always felt it wasn't good enough to earn the love I so longed for. I actually believed that I had to earn love by doing the right things or by doing whatever anyone asked me to do. That wasn't very good as I grew older because then I began to do what boys asked me to do in order to get the love for which I yearned. That took me down a path from which I had to be rescued. But who was there to rescue me?

How I longed for you, Mommy. How I longed for a hug, for you to tell me you loved me. Oh, if only I had heard those words even once, maybe that empty place inside of me would have been filled and I might have discovered what love really is.

Part of this is my story. Is part of it yours?

How did I get healed from the brokenness in my life? I got healed by the One who said that He would not forget me. The One who has my name engraved in the palms of His hands.

> *Can a mother forget the baby at her breast*
> *and have no compassion on the child she has borne?*
> *Though she may forget,*
> *I will never forget you!*
> *See, I have engraved you on the palms of my hands.*
> *(Isaiah 49:15, 16 NIV)*

God remembered.

CHAPTER TWO
The Beginning

Where does healing begin? So much hurt, pain, disappointment. For me it began at the beginning, a place I didn't know that I needed to go, a place I didn't even know existed.

When I was growing up, I attended Sunday School and church fairly regularly. Why didn't I hear someone say, "Ask Jesus to come into your heart. Ask Him to be Lord of your life"? Was I not hearing, or was the message not sent? I'm not sure what it was. I only know that it wasn't until I was in my thirties, married, with children, and feeling like a complete and total failure as a wife and mother that I cried out in desperation to God. "God, if You are there, please take over my life. I've made such a mess of it. I need help. Help, Lord, help!"

I didn't see flashing lights. I felt a sense of peace in the midst of the storm. That was the beginning of my journey with Jesus. There was a longing in my spirit to know more. Before that day, I thought people who carried Bibles around were a bit strange. After that day, the Bible became my constant companion as the hunger in me grew to know more of Him. But it was only the beginning of a long journey of discovery of what it means to walk with Him.

That was the beginning of my spiritual journey and the first step to healing the brokenness in my life, but that is not the beginning to which I referred.

The healing of my relationship with my mother came in unexpected ways. I had a fairly good relationship with my mother before she died, but I discovered that there was a deep hurt buried inside of me that I knew nothing about.

Did it ever occur to you that some of the attitudes and behaviors in your life may be connected to that time before you were born or at your birth? Sounds strange doesn't it? Studies have been done that indicate that a child in utero is sensitive to what is going on in their surroundings. I was told that, but was skeptical until I experienced some deep inner healing as a woman prayed for me.

I was in a small prayer group. A guest had been invited to come and pray healing prayers with the group, leading us from conception to birth. That was the focus of the evening. As she prayed, she began with conception and moved month by month through the gestation period asking Jesus to reveal those places where some trauma may have occurred. I went along with it, not even believing anything was going to happen or change.

When she reached the point of the actual birth, I had my eyes closed. In my mind's eye, I saw myself being born and saw my mother handing me to my father. The feelings that went along with that were extremely painful. The "perception" I had was that my mother was giving me to my father to take care of. My life experience validated that, as my father was the nurturing parent in my life. The feelings I had at that moment were that she didn't want to "have to" take care of me—a feeling of rejection. I started to weep.

The prayer minister came to me and began to pray, "Jesus, reveal the truth to Migsie."

She prayed quietly for some time. As I continued to keep my eyes closed, I saw a different picture. I saw my mother handing me to Jesus, not my father—an act of love, not rejection. I can't describe the healing that occurred in those moments.

"My mother loved me, she didn't reject me!" Tears flowed, but they were tears of joy, not of sorrow. This was a step in the healing of my brokenness, but only the beginning of a lifetime of layers of hurt and pain being peeled away by the One who:

... created my inmost being
Who knit me together in my mother's womb.

His Word also says:

My frame was not hidden from You
When I was made in the secret place.

Do you know anything about that period in your life?
Were your parents married when you were conceived?
Were you wanted?
Was there strife surrounding your mother's pregnancy?
Was there anger, resentment, condemnation?
Was there fear?
Was your mother ill at any time during that period?
Were you the "right" gender, according to your parents?
(You were, according to your heavenly Father.)

Could this be a place where you need some healing?

For you created my inmost being;
You knit me together in my mother's womb.
I praise you because I am fearfully and
wonderfully made;
I know that full well.
My frame was not hidden from You
When I was made in the secret place.
When I was woven together in the depths of earth,
Your eyes saw my unformed body
All the days ordained for me
Were written in your book before one of them came to be.
(Psalm 139:13–16 NIV)

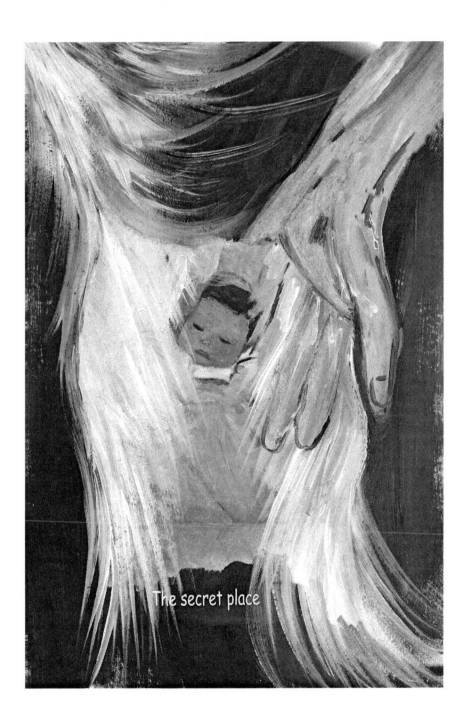

The secret place

CHAPTER THREE
Violated

I was just six years old. We had friends of the family who would babysit my brother and me on different occasions. I don't remember when it first started, I only remember the events and the shame that accompanied them.

I was only six years old when he asked me to climb into bed with him. I thought it was just to cuddle me before I drifted off to sleep. I was wrong! Here was an authority figure whom I loved and respected, violating my body, violating my trust. I was a very confused little girl. Feelings were stirred up in me that up until that time, I knew nothing about. Some of those feelings were nice feelings. What was happening to me? What was I supposed to do?

I wanted my mommy. I wanted to tell her, but I was afraid. How could she do that to me, leave me with him? Didn't she know what he was like?

He told me not to tell anyone. Why not? It must be bad. Whatever was happening had to be bad. New feelings rose up in me, feelings of fear. I was afraid to tell anyone. There were also feelings of guilt and shame. Whatever I was doing was wrong. How tormented this little girl came to be.

I was sixty years old when I was asked to speak to a women's group on *The Healing of Damaged Emotions*, based on the book written by David Seamans.[1] As I was praying and preparing my message, I felt the Lord told me to tell about my sexual abuse. My response to God: "I can't tell that. I've never told anyone that!" But I was convicted. The next morning as I was having breakfast with my husband, I told him about my sexual abuse. That was the first time those words had ever left my lips. With that confession came an avalanche of tears. The sobbing went on and on and on. I felt like I was being purged of a poison that had killed my innocence and robbed my childhood of the delight and joys I should have known—a sense of worth and value. I had been in bondage, in a prison, and didn't know it, until the door was opened, the truth was out, and I was set free!

I did share that story with those women and many others. In the sharing, I have seen countless others come to a new sense of freedom and peace because the lies they had believed were exposed and the truth set them free.

We all have secrets, things we may have done or experienced that we don't want anyone to know about, but as we confess them to a trusted friend or counselor and to God (He already knows anyway), we will experience a release and a freedom we have never known before. He wants you to trust Him with the truth.

Then you will know the truth, and the truth will set you free.
(John 8:32 NIV)

Confession is a major step toward healing. Light is brought into the dark places of our lives. The secrets are out, and we can no longer be tormented by the guilt, shame and condemnation we have carried. A new kind of freedom is experienced.

I didn't realize that that was just a step in my healing. The Lord had some more work to do on the inside of me.

You may have never heard of the ministry of "inner healing" or the healing of memories. I hadn't until the experience I shared in regard to my birth, but I was soon to discover the depth of healing that can come through trusting in the One who reminds us in His Word:

O Lord, You have searched me and know me.
You know when I sit down and when I rise;
You perceive my thoughts from afar.
You discern my going out and my lying down;
You are familiar with all my ways
Before a word is on my tongue
You know it completely, O Lord.

You hem me in—behind and before;
You have laid your hand upon me
Such knowledge is too wonderful for me,
Too lofty for me to attain.

Where can I go from your Spirit
Where can I flee from your presence?
If I go up to the heavens, you are there;
If I make my bed in the depths, you are there.
If I rise on the wings of the dawn,
If I settle on the far side of the sea,
Even there your hand will guide me
Your right hand will hold me fast.

If I say, "Surely the darkness will hide me
And the light become night around me,"
Even the darkness will not be dark to you:
The night will shine like the day,
For darkness is as light to you.

Then it goes on to say:

Search me, O God, and know my heart;
Test me and know my anxious thoughts.
See if there is any offensive way in me,
And lead me in the way everlasting.
(Psalm 139:1–12, 23–24 NIV)

He already knows all about you.

I attended a conference led by Norma Dearing who has been affiliated with Christian Healing Ministries in Jacksonville, Florida. She was teaching on "Inner Healing." At one point she asked us to bow our heads and to ask Jesus what place He wanted to heal that day. As I prayed and waited on the Lord (waiting is hard, but important), He revealed Himself to me in my spirit. I saw Him take me to the place where I had been sexually abused. I didn't want to go there because I felt so much shame, but I saw Him lovingly lift me out of the bed of my perpetrator and take me to my own bed. He sat beside me comforting me until I fell asleep. I felt such love, acceptance, and peace. Another layer of hurt and pain fell away.

I experienced a deeper healing of this experience that I will share in a later chapter. But there had been other situations in my life where there had been an invasion into the tender parts of my spirit.

Once more as I prayed, He revealed another place He wanted to heal. In my spirit I saw Him take me to a bedroom. I must have been only about four years old. A man came into the room. I think that he was someone who had come to check something in the house, but he approached me, pushed me down on the bed, spread my legs apart, and "checked me out." I did not see, nor do I remember him doing anything more than that, but it was a memory I could not erase from my mind.

As I prayed for the healing of that memory, I saw Jesus lift me up in His arms. He hugged me and held me as I cried in His arms. I was so afraid, but He comforted me and turned me toward the man. I couldn't see his face, but what I did see was a millstone hanging around his neck. It revealed to me that he was not going to go unpunished. Jesus was going to take care of him and I didn't have to be afraid. I could trust Him to take care of any injustice toward me. He brought this scripture to my mind:

It would be better for him if a millstone were hung around his neck ,and he were thrown into the sea, than that he should offend one of these little ones.
(Luke 17:2, NKJV)

Another time as I prayed and asked Jesus if there were an area He wanted to heal, the memory of a time when I was probably twelve years old and was in junior high school came to mind.

I was having lunch in the cafeteria when two boys came up next to me and dropped a sanitary napkin next to my chair and then said rather loudly, "Hey, Migsie, you dropped something." I looked down

15

and saw what they had dropped—and so did a number of others.

I was mortified! You can imagine how a girl that age felt, so influenced by what others thought and wanting so much to fit in and be cool. I didn't realize that it had hurt me as much as it did, until Jesus returned me to that place, the tears came, and the pain returned.

But what a gracious and loving God we have. I saw Jesus ushering the two boys away. Then I saw Him come to me. He stood behind me and held the chair for me as I stood up as if I were someone special.

He then put His arm around me and walked with me down through a row of tables crowded with children. All eyes turned to watch us as we left. I felt like He was saying to me,

"You're mine and you are very special." He made me feel that way, and I felt like all those who were watching were envious of me being escorted by Jesus.

As we walked out I turned around and said, "What about that sanitary napkin on the floor?" He said, "It's just like spilled milk," and smiled.

Then I saw an angel standing there with a mop. What seemed funny to me was that it wasn't a new, clean mop, it was a soiled one, indicating to me that the angel was used to cleaning up dirty spills!

Many are the afflictions of the righteous,
But the Lord delivers him out of them all.
(Psalm 34:19 NKJV)

He had healed me of another painful memory.

As I write this I realize that you may be saying to yourself, "I can't see anything when I pray. What do you mean, 'see Jesus'?"

"When Jesus' Holy Spirit is at the core of your being, He can reveal Himself to you any way He chooses. It may not be in pictures, but thoughts He plants in your mind. You may just have a sense of His presence, His warmth, His love. You may have a revelation where lights come on for you in an area of life you may be struggling. He knows all about you, and He knows the best way to communicate with you" (spoken by Norma Dearing at a Healing Prayer Conference).[2]

Only recently He gave me a new revelation. So often healing has been likened to peeling off the layers of an onion. Healing does takes place layer by layer, but what He revealed to me is that the healing begins from the inside out. When we ask Jesus to come into our hearts, His Holy Spirit dwells in us and is at the core of our being—the core of the onion. As we seek Him, the layers begin to fall away, like a "blooming onion." We begin to "bloom" the way He intended.

The experiences I have shared may appear as nothing to you compared to the horrors of abuse that you may have experienced. I understand that, but I know that God has no favorites (Acts 10:34, Romans 2:11 NIV). What He did for me, He wants to do for you. He is not going to let those who have violated you go unpunished. He is a just God, and His Word says:

> *Vengeance is Mine*
> *It is Mine to avenge. I will repay*
> *(Deut. 32:35 NKJV, NIV)*

and

> *If the Son sets you free, you will be free indeed.*
> *(John 8:36 NIV)*

My child,
Do you think for one minute that I am not angry about what was
done to you?
Yes, I know it was done to you.
And yet, in your innocence, you blamed yourself.
I heard your cry, and it grieved me that I couldn't just pluck you out
of that situation.
You say, "Why, Lord, why, when You can do anything.?
My child, I had to give the right to choose to My people.
By doing that I limited My actions, but I did not limit My presence.

"Things that cause people to sin are bound to come, but woe to that person through whom they come. It would be better for him to be thrown into the sea with a millstone tied around his neck than for him to cause one of these little ones to sin" (Luke 17:1,2 NIV).
These are My words.
These are My feelings.
You are My child, My little one, and I am a just God
And I will pay back trouble to those who trouble you (2 Thess. 1:6 NIV).
It is never My will that harm should come to anyone
And especially to you, My child.
I desire only good for you.
But there is one who seeks to harm you
And he used those who don't know Me to bring oppression and suffering to you.
There is so much you don't see or understand, but as you draw near to Me, I will teach you.
As you read My Word,
l will reveal those things to you
For that is My good pleasure (Matt. 11:25, 26 NIV).
Trust Me with your life.
For I know the plans I have for you.
Plans to prosper you and not to harm you,
Plans to give you hope and a future.
You will seek me and find Me when you seek Me with all your heart.
I will be found by you (Jeremiah 29:11, 13 NIV).

Love, Your Heavenly Father

Seek Him with all your heart. Wait for Him to reveal Himself to you. Listen. He is longing for you to come to Him.

Come to Me all you who labor and are heavy laden, and I will give you rest.
(Matthew 11:28 NKJV)

I sought the Lord, and he answered me;

He delivered me from all my fears.
Those who look to him are radiant:
Their faces are never covered with shame.
(Psalm 34:4, 5 NIV)

He wants to remove all of that shame and see your face radiant once more and your heart filled with joy and laughter—yes, laughter:

So those who went off with heavy hearts
Will come home laughing, with armloads of blessing.
(Psalm 126:6 TMSG)

CHAPTER FOUR
Who Was She?

Who was your mom?

One of the most significant areas of healing in the women who attended the "Mommy" class came as they gained a new perspective and a greater understanding of their mother's lives and life experiences.

Just as every child has a story, so does every mother. What is her story? What kind of life did she lead while she was growing up? What were the hurts, pain, and disappointments that impacted and formed her life?

As you read these stories perhaps you will gain some insights and a greater understanding of the mother who gave you life. Hopefully, your perception of her will change and make a pathway to forgiveness and deep healing in you.

Jennifer's Story

She was single, nineteen years old, and pregnant. She had a good job, but her boss said that if she were pregnant and it became obvious, that she would have to let her go. "It wouldn't look good for the company." The father of the child wasn't interested in having her keep the baby. She didn't want to be pregnant at that time in her life, but she was. The thoughts of having an abortion created a conflict between her circumstances and her values. What should she do?

When she called a doctor to inquire about an abortion, he told her that he didn't believe in abortions and had the feeling that she wasn't convinced that that was what she wanted either. He offered to care for her at no charge. She felt like that was divine intervention, and from that point on was determined to keep the baby that was growing inside of her.

When she told the father of the baby of her decision, he gave her a $100 and she never heard from him again.

She then looked to her family, who at first seemed supportive, but the opinion of others seemed to influence them in such a way that they were not then openly supportive of her.

She felt alone in her decision. She was feeling condemned by others and began to beat up on herself, wondering if she could ever be forgiven.

She was angry at God. How could she feel so alone at a time like this? Where was He anyway? "Do you not hear me?" was her cry. But as she cried out to Him, she felt a shift in her focus from herself to her baby. Her thoughts: "Okay, God. I might be dead to you, but my baby is innocent." She prayed that God would take care of her child.

Later, as she looked back on this time, she could see God's hand upon her, leading her through this season of her life. But at that moment, at least, the welfare of the baby became of prime importance to her.

She began to be concerned about the child's health and took a greater responsibility in caring for herself, moving away from destructive habits.

She continued to work until her boss said she could work no longer, but in the meantime a friend came into her life. It was someone she hadn't known before, but someone who didn't condemn or judge her, who walked beside through the days ahead. She attended birthing classes with her and when she lost her job, her friend took her in.

It was during this time that she was feeling that she had nothing to offer this baby, that she didn't know how she could raise a child, and that what she really wanted was what was best for her child. She started to consider adoption.

Once Jennifer made that decision, she felt she needed to learn all she could about adoption. She said she was "feeling the most responsible she had ever been."

She attended an adoption support group and ultimately met with a couple who were kind, humble, and sincere, who wanted so much to adopt a baby. They seemed to understand her pain as they had experienced so much pain in pursuit of having a family of their own.

She didn't feel she could make any promises to them at that

time because she didn't know how she would feel after the birth, but she pursued a relationship with them.

Jennifer spent the next few months getting to know them. They picked out a name together and she made them promise that they would love him every day, that they would tell him he was adopted, that they would not lose touch with her in case of some emergency, that they would send her pictures every month for the first year and every year after that and that they would bring him to her if ever and whenever he asked about her.

Even after they agreed, she still wasn't sure she could give him up. "I wanted to protect him all my life."

The day came for her son to be born. He was placed in her arms and she was overcome with love and joy, "the miracle of life resting in my arms." The adoptive family came to visit. She spent two days feeding, changing, holding, hugging, kissing, and saying goodbye. It was during those two days that she made the decision that she felt was the right and best decision for her son.

"To this day it is the hardest choice I've ever made and the hardest thing I've ever done."

She wrote this letter to be given to her son.

Dear Son,

Well, you're finally here! So many people were excited about you coming, it's hard to believe we did it and you're here in the big world.

I think you and I made a great team while we were together. I want you to know what a wonderful difference you've made in my life. By carrying you in my belly and so close to my heart for nine months, I learned what true love is all about.

When you were born, the nurse cleaned you up and then handed you to me. You lay, wrapped in a blanket, on my chest. You didn't cry, but just looked at me and listened to me talk to you. You smiled. You recognized my voice. It was the most incredible moment of my life, and you're the one who gave that moment to me. Although you won't remember it, we shared it, and it will be in my heart forever. Even though we won't be together under one roof, we'll be together under one heaven, and I just know that if we both keep God close to our hearts He will continue to watch over us the way He did during this time in our lives.

Leaving the hospital tomorrow will be the hardest thing I've ever done. As I write this letter you're lying in bed next to me. It feels so good to hold you and I can't imagine not holding you again after tomorrow. I'm very scared to leave you, because I know my heart is going to break. But I am happy for you, you're a lot more fortunate than most, you have love coming from all directions: your (adoptive) brother, grandparents, your mother and your father is the love you will see every day and that's very special. But you also have me, and that's the love I hope you'll feel every day. I know you will.

I hope as you grow you will learn to be an unselfish, caring, and loving young man, just like the person I've come to know in your father. Listen to him and learn from him, and you will grow to be a very happy person.

I will be praying for you every day. If you ever want to see me, I want to see you. Just let me know.

I love you so very much. I love you so much my heart is aching. We'll say our goodbyes tonight. Your mother and father will be here in the morning to take you home. Maybe someday we'll say hello again. I hope we do. I love you!

Your mother,
Jennifer

Her son went home in the arms of another. She left the hospital with empty arms and an "intolerable aching" in her heart. She said she "felt like someone had pulled out my guts." In her room by herself she began to rock and to wail, "God help me!"

He did. She felt His touch and heard Him say, "I understand. I gave up my Son, too."

The self loathing was gone! She said, "It was as if God reached into my heart, and finally I stood strong and knew that I had made the right choice. I could see that life was not always about me."

Who was your mother? What path did she take in her walk of life? What circumstances surrounded your conception? What obstacles did she have to overcome?

Were you adopted? Did you feel like you were not wanted, were rejected by someone who was supposed to love you, take care of you? Does that stir up some anger, some hurt, some pain? Do you feel like you were abandoned? Is there that nagging question in your mind and heart, "Why, Mommy, why? Why did you leave me?" Is there a deep longing to know and to understand that part of your life, to have that pain in your heart healed?

Perhaps, just perhaps, she really did want you. Perhaps, just perhaps, she thought she was loving you best by giving you to someone who could care for you in a way she could not. Perhaps, just perhaps, giving you up was one of the most painful experiences of her life.

Bonnie's Story

[Bonnie writes:] Growing up in a large family, I "got lost." I can remember going through photo albums at home with relatives and never seeing a baby picture of Bonnie. There were plenty for the sisters before and after me. As a little girl, I thought that maybe I was too ugly for them to take my picture. I later found out that I had a broken arm that would not heal properly, so it was wrapped in a bandage for a long time. I don't know if that excuse was supposed to make me feel better, but regardless of the excuse, the damage had already been done. I thought that I wasn't pretty enough for pictures, so I tended to avoid them from that point on.

I still don't know how my arm was broken. My mother came home from work to find me screaming and my two oldest siblings, who were only nine and ten at the time, blaming each other for either dropping or stepping on me. I don't think my mom really wanted to know because she was so familiar with violence herself. My biological father was an alcoholic, addicted to a drug that ended his life when I was six years old. One of the very few memories I have of him he was dragging my mother across the kitchen floor by her hair and then pounding his fist into her head. My mom eventually escaped him, leaving three of us girls behind while the older two siblings disappeared. I can't remember a time when we have ever all been together. I've always thought they "got lost," too.

After my father died, we went to live with my mother and her new husband. He was the one who told us that our father was gone. I remember being so scared—of my stepfather and what he was telling me—and looked toward my mother for comfort, only to find her crying over her knitting for the baby boy in her belly. I now had two more stepsiblings, and this child would be number eight. "She had so many children, she didn't know what to do" is a familiar nursery rhyme. I don't think my mother ever knew what to do with me, or for me. I was lost somewhere in the middle of this family.

When asked to recall my life as a little girl, I am filled with happy memories of laying with my baby brother, my best friend next door, and escapes to the nicer homes of my aunts and uncles. There are also the less pleasant memories of moving away from my best friend, punishments doled out by a strict father, and the harmful words of parents who didn't know how to handle the daily challenges of life. I too suffered from the sexual offenses of a family member who shall remain nameless because I still struggle with the shame of it all.

Although my parents did not go to church themselves (one recovering from a strict religious upbringing and the other an exiled, divorced Catholic), they did have the foresight to send my sisters and me to services and Sunday school each week. I always thought it was because they wanted us out of the house for a couple of hours. I was "saved" at the age of twelve, but didn't understand what it all meant. It was in my Baptist upbringing that I learned about the wrath of God and love of Jesus—a mixed message that ultimately pushed me away from church as soon as I was old enough to make excuses not to go. Thus, I was even lost to God.

Then I really got lost. By the time I was seventeen years old, I'd learned to fend for myself and moved out on my own. I became an independent woman of the '90s, making my own money and spending it on every pleasure available to fill the void of abandonment I'd carried most of my life. But God didn't give up on this sheep. He sent many people onto my path to be a parent to me: my first boss who helped me establish credit and learn the value of money; my female co-workers who taught me how to be a lady; and one special woman who saw in me the gift of love for children, which led to a position as a Sunday school teacher.

From a professional standpoint, I was doing wonderfully. When compared to most of my siblings, I was the one who had it made. Although I was gaining some fulfillment spiritually, it was still through the eyes of a child. From a personal standpoint, I was still confused, lonely, and lost. I craved attention and sought it in all the wrong places. I found myself so desperate for love that I settled for relationships in which I could overlook indiscretions and unhealthy habits, ultimately settling for a handsome young man with a drinking habit (sound familiar?).

Shortly after his second DUI, I became ill and called my mom to take me to the doctor. When she arrived at my apartment, I tried to talk to her about my fear that he was an alcoholic and admitted to seeing a psychologist for the last few months. But she wouldn't talk about any of it, rushing me out of the room and to the doctor's. I ended up in the hospital that day, diagnosed with bulimia (something I never told my psychologist about) and needing to be fed intravenously. When my fiancé showed up that night, my mother left me in his care, and she and I have never spoken about it.

Realizing that this relationship would never work, I got lost—yet again. In addition to ending my engagement, I left my Sunday school post, feeling that if I had really been a part of that church, these things would never have happened to me. With the help of a few more parental figures, friends who were a bit closer to the true me, I began to seek a healthier path to emotional fulfillment. Most of these came in the form of books. I became an avid reader of self-help material, learning to work through my fears and frustrations through journaling.

Seeking a deeper understanding and knowing there was much more I needed to fill the void in my heart, I also started looking for alternatives for my spiritual fulfillment other than my religious experiences of the past. I checked out *Seacoast Church*, casually attending services when they were convenient, enjoying the praise and worship, and slowly getting fed by the message. I had my own ideas about religion and God, though, and continued to entertain the alternatives to Christ such as Buddhism and reincarnation, until 9/11, when the world's religions became a focal point of a lot of lives. I remember being in the store with my mother when the announcement came over the radio that we were going to war. My youngest brother had just gotten out of army boot camp and I tried to talk to my mom about our mutual fears. She again refused, and I again withdrew.

I, along with many other wayward Christians, began to take my spiritual path a bit more seriously after that. I signed up for the growth track and started doing home Bible studies with friends whose faith had also deepened by joining me at our church. God sent another person into my life, a wonderful man who was willing to partner with me on a quest toward God—someone with whom I could share the amazing things that God was doing in my life by changing my heart and mind. Together, we recommitted our lives to Christ and publicly acknowledged Him as our Lord and Savior at a water baptism—just one more step in my journey home.

When the initial advertisements for the "*Where Were You, Mommy?*" classes were published, I was curious, but held off on signing up. Years of therapy had already taught me that I had issues with my mother and father, and I was frankly tired of battling with the feelings of rejection and hurt. I had recently "detached" from my family, and was busy making new friends at church. But as my relationship with my friend grew more serious and the desire to give back to the church intensified, I knew that I would have to deal more effectively with this area of my life if I wanted a family of my own.

Through hearing personal testimonials similar to my history, I was drawn into a group of women who opened my eyes and heart to the power of God's healing grace. I had already known that my feelings of loss and abandonment were natural and acceptable. But never before had I been challenged to look at my parents not through the eyes of a child, but as an adult. Never before had I been asked to look through their eyes at their own life. Never before had it been suggested that I look at them through God's eyes. As my mind began to slowly process this new information, my heart was opened. As a group, we dealt lovingly with a new kind of pain and anguish—that which comes from letting go of bitterness and disappointments (things that have kept me from fully experiencing God's love) to forgive.

I am still my parent's child, so I am learning to re-attach to my family. With the help of my younger sister in North Carolina, who is also very involved with her own church, we are finding ways to heal our family with Christ as our guide. But even today, I find myself asking "Where are you, Mom?" In announcing my engagement, I looked to her for love, encouragement, and support, but found none. My mother hasn't changed, but I have, so I continue to forgive, to look through another pair of eyes, and then I find that love and support from God.

Through both the "Mommy" class and my Encounter weekend, I have learned so much about myself and know that I am not alone in some of what I've experienced. But God has His purpose, and I look forward to how He will use my life from this point forward.

Is there something in Bonnie's story that rings true in your life? Did you feel lost in your own family, like no one cared about you? Did you feel like other siblings were favored? Were there feelings of jealousy, competition, always wanting someone to notice you, who you were, and what you were doing and needing? When you tried to share your concerns, your fears, did your mommy take time to listen to you, or was she missing?

As an adult are you still looking for ways to fill that void in your life, the little girl inside of you, still longing to be noticed? Are you seeking love, fulfillment, acceptance in all the wrong places?

Did you ever wonder why your mom didn't or perhaps couldn't

respond to you in the way you so longed for? Was she overwhelmed by the demands on her? Were there family financial concerns? Was she needing to feel loved and valued by someone?

Debbie's Story

[Debbie writes:] I am the oldest of three sisters. My daddy was in the Air Force, which took us to several different cities in my growing up years. My mom stayed at home. She was strict and made sure we behaved well.

Our Christmases were what I lived for. It was the happiest time of the year. My mom would get caught up in the holiday spirit. She'd play Christmas carols of Johnny Mathis and Bing Crosby. She would spend hours decorating our home and spend much time in the kitchen baking lots of goodies.

She was an excellent seamstress and sewed most of our clothes. I recall a special moment when one Christmas morning I received a gift, one I would always remember. My mom had made doll clothes for my favorite doll, but not just plain doll clothes. She had taken the time to embellish those clothes with tiny stitches. It made me feel so special. We seemed to be the normal family.

To my father, we girls were the apples of his eye. I could crawl up in his lap, snuggle close and feel secure and that no matter what happened my daddy would always be my "knight in shining armor." He had a deep, sincere love for us girls that showed through the smile in his blue eyes. He always made sure we saw every Disney movie that came to the silver screen. My favorite? *Cinderella*.

As time went on my mom became lonely as the military continued to send my father overseas, leaving us behind. My mom became involved with several men during that time, but I was never aware of it until I became older.

Mom often looked for peace and found her place in the Catholic church where she sang in the choir. Yet, she was unsettled in her life. Longing for fulfillment, she stumbled into transcendental meditation, believing this would bring her inner peace. She became so involved in transcendental meditation she left the Catholic church behind.

As time went on she divorced my father for reasons of her own, believing that they were incompatible. I, being the one for the underdog, went with my father. My two sisters followed.

My world seemed to shatter as I watched my dad grieve. Our first Christmas without Mom was unbearable. My dad cried most of the day, causing me to dislike my mom all the more.

Daddy, my two sisters, and I would soon move on. We went for years not seeing my mom. She closed the door on us as she went ever deeper into the occult.

My father remarried again, but it didn't seem for love. I think he thought this woman would take care of his girls. His plans of blending us were sifted like wheat. Just as soon as the wedding vows were spoken, my father's new wife wanted no part in his three girls as she had four children of her own. She began making plans to move me and my sisters out of their new life together, and one by one she succeeded. We were no longer the sparkle in my daddy's eye. He had a new family. With feelings of abandonment and rejection, not only from my mom but also now from my father (whom I trusted and thought loved me), resentment, unknowingly, snuck in on me.

I soon married a wonderful man, who I truly believe was God sent. I decided early on that my home would be filled with love and that my children would never feel the pain of being abandoned. I watched Leave it to Beaver (a television show in the early '60's), and made June Cleaver my role model.

After our first child was born, I began to feel I was missing something. I needed a mother or a father. I wanted someone there for me to encourage me, to bring me hope when life wasn't fair.

I soon began working at a Baptist church as the church secretary and found the strength I needed through the pastor. He was a strong leader, a father himself; he taught me to lean on, rely on, and put my trust in God. I was learning to find comfort.

Our family began to grow, and I chose to stay at home with our now three boys. I put my whole self into the boys and trusted God with everything in my life. But I was missing something. I soon discovered that unforgiveness was holding me back.

A friend took me to a women's group in my church. I called it my "mommy" group. There I learned God's grace. The beautiful lady in charge walked each of us through a cleansing, walking me through forgiveness for my mom. The ministry was healing for me like no other. I was able to move on, not hating my mom anymore, not feeling left out anymore, but feeling sorry for my mom because she had missed so much of life with her girls.

I began to seek God, praying that my mom would come back into my life. Within the year my mom began to visit us. Then she did something I never thought possible. She broke down and cried and told me how sorry she was for running away from her children. Would I forgive her? And I did.

Her time with me at first wasn't what I had envisioned. I had to trust and lean on God, expecting and knowing He has a good plan for my life. Several years came and went, and when my mom turned seventy, it happened! My mom came to know the Lord!

I am learning anew who this person is I call "Mom." The road hasn't been easy, but I can see God's hand moving as I trust Him with each new day. My mom and I are a little closer at becoming the mother and daughter He intended us to be. When I think of Isaiah 30:18 (NIV), "The Lord longs to be gracious to you; he rises to show you compassion. For the Lord is a God of justice. Blessed are all those who wait for him," I am reminded of a God who knows the desires of my heart. He has been so gracious to me. He has shown me compassion and His justice as I have waited for him. He saw into my heart and made my desires a reality.

Debbie had a normal happy family early on in her life, but her parents made decisions that deeply impacted her sense of security and wellbeing. Divorce can do that! All of a sudden those you came to depend on and trust are no longer a part of your everyday life. Feelings of hurt, resentment, anger, and bitterness start to make a home in your heart, and you don't know how to deal with all that. Does some of this ring true for you? Do you ever wonder how you can ever be healed of all that hurt and pain?

Debbie found some of those answers as she pursued the One who could bring healing and restoration to her brokenness. He gave her eyes to see the loneliness and sadness of her mother's life, and compassion filled Debbie's heart as her mother reentered her life.

Penny's Story

[Penny writes:] My mother was an alcoholic. As far back as I can remember there were many men in her life. I was brought up in bars. Bars were almost nightly "homes" for me. Many men were always there.

Violence and abuse of all kinds were just a daily part of life for me. The nights were worse.

I can remember going with my mother to her sister's house once, and after a lot of arguing, my aunt Louise got a brush to brush my hair. It was very painful. Finally she had to cut it off at the scalp, all the way around because it was so "matted" from not being brushed in so long. I might have been three or four years old then.

My mother finally married an alcoholic. He was extremely violent. Most of the time my mother was unrecognizable due to the severe beatings he would give her. They stayed drunk always, day and night. There was rarely any food, although once in a while a pack of bologna would be in the refrigerator. But they always, day and night, had their beer.

I can remember eating the neighbor's dog food sometimes. My mother and her husband gave me beer a lot, too (maybe to make me sleep more?).

They also taught me how to smoke. They would light the cigarettes for me because I wasn't able to light the matches myself, but finally they taught me how to do that, too.

All this dysfunction led me to a life of extreme anger and rage toward my mother. Why? How could she?

Many times she would take me to a baby sitter and promise to see me in a few hours and she simply wouldn't come back. I ended up in foster homes, police stations, and sometimes in worse situations than even being at home.

She would tell me that if I were dead, her life would be good, and that I was the cause of all her problems. Her solution to life was my death, so my first serious suicide attempt was at about age five. [Editor's Note: When I asked Penny how she even knew how to commit suicide, she told me that her grandmother had told her to never take her mother's medicine or it would kill her—so she took her mother's medicine.] I can't even count the ones since then. I won't continue, but there's a whole lot more I could say about my childhood.

This I share with you to give you an idea that if you've ever wondered why your mother wasn't there for you, I understand how you feel, but more important than where we have been is where we end up. I can honestly tell you that I've found the answer to being complete and total—every day and every night peace and serenity is in my life. My peace is not temporary, like the world offers. It's not something that comes and goes with my moods or is conditional upon outside circumstances. When it comes to inner turmoil and rage against my mother, that part of me is simply gone.

All the unforgiveness I've had my whole life has now been filled with total forgiveness and tenderness towards her. But it didn't happen until I started crying out to Jesus to show me if He was real or not. I wanted to believe in Him, but the fact was I didn't. I couldn't believe in another disappointing Santa Claus story. I didn't have it in me to put effort in to anything else or anyone else for nothing. So I told Him, "If you are real, explain this scripture to me which, by the way, Jesus, makes no sense whatsoever."

And He [Jesus] said to them. "Assuredly, I say to you that there are some standing here who will not taste death [die] till they see the kingdom of God present with power."
(Mark 9:1 NKJV)

I said, "If you are really God and real, it shouldn't be too hard for you to explain that to me. Just You and me without anyone else."

I almost "passed out" when He did explain it. You don't have to die to see the kingdom of God. He could be experienced in this lifetime as well as after you die. He's here and available now. It isn't just about heaven, it's about now! Then I looked further into the Bible, because at that point I knew beyond any doubt that He was real and alive and active.

I didn't realize until later that He'd been with me even when I wasn't "seeking Him." I had seen a movie, *The Lord of the Rings*, sometime before all this happened (all three of the movies). The Lord used this movie in amazing ways in my life to start my permanent forgiveness of my mother. It made me see how much she was in bondage and that she'd finally lost all control over her own life. "The ring" (control of the dark side) had consumed her. She didn't ever get the wonderful opportunity (through Jesus) that I had, for some unknown reason, to be freed from her own bondage. She died long before her physical death without any escape from her personal "hell." She never knew the only escape—my precious Jesus, who came to set the captives free. I can't say that I fully understand why I was given this priceless gift, but I know that God's Word says that

He is "no respecter of persons." Anyone who seeks Him will find Him (Jeremiah 29:13, 14).

I discovered that finding Him is the one and only key to freedom. I had tried everything else, much to my disappointment. But in Him there is no disappointment—only relief, contentment, freedom, life. He is the way, the truth, and the life. And when He sets you free, you will be free indeed.

As you reflect on Penny's life, do you see yourself anywhere? Her early childhood was couched in violence, neglect, abandonment, and many moments of despair, when she felt the only relief would come from death. The mother who should have been a positive role model for her child introduced her to a life of degradation through her lifestyle of drinking, lust, irresponsibility, and neglect. But Penny's life has been a journey from the depths of despair to new hope as she has come to see the woundedness of her mother through the eyes of the One who has helped her release her mom and the events of the past and has brought her to a place of joy and peace.

My Story

My story began long before I was born, with my mother's story. The year was 1918, and the swine flu was running rampant in the United States. My mother was only eight years old when she had to look through a window to say her goodbyes to her dead mother, a victim of that dread disease. What a terrible loss for that young child!

Her father remarried and she, like Cinderella, had a stepmother and stepsisters who didn't show her the same kind of love her mother had shown. Her father died, and her stepmother chose not to keep her.

Her grandmother took her in. She was raised by her grandmother and aunts until she was old enough to go to nursing school. It was then that her only sibling, a brother, died of pneumonia. Heartbroken, she left school and went to be a nanny for her cousins.

How do you survive all those losses? Most likely because of the fears of loss, abandonment, and rejection, she had to take an unusual amount of responsibility for herself. With that came a need to control. If she didn't take control, something bad might happen. Fear had a grip on her. Control had a grip on me.

Only recently have I come to understand my mother's need to control my life. For years I carried resentment toward her, not understanding what lay behind that need to control.

As I grew up, I was afraid not to please her. She made so many decisions for me that it took me years to discover who I really was. I was what she wanted me to be and what everyone else wanted me to be. I became a "people pleaser."

It is only as I have grown in my relationship with the Lord that my desire to please Him has grown and the desire to please others has lessened. But it is still a challenge for me, and I have to keep reminding myself whom it is I choose to please.

I had to forgive my mother, not only for that control, but for those many, many disappointments I experienced throughout my life. I had many wonderful moments with my mom, but there were some painful moments as well.

She became a working mom, and there were many times when I saw very little of her. (Only as an adult could I understand her need to work to keep our family afloat.) I longed for her to be at those special events in my life, to be able to look out in the audience and see her face, to hear words of affirmation and encouragement that, coming from her, would mean the world to me. Yes, there was a little girl saying, "Look at me, Mommy. Did I do okay?" I wanted so much to please her.

As I look back on my life, I know my mother loved me. But through a little girl's eyes, I felt she favored my brother. It wasn't until I was in my thirties that I finally felt I had "made it" in her eyes. Even though I knew my mom loved me, there were some areas of wounding that needed healing.

"In some sense every parent does love their children. But some parents are too broken to love them well and others are barely able to love them at all" (*The Shack*).[3]

Mary Pytches, in her book *Dying to Change*,[4] says this: "A child's experience influences him to a greater degree than anything else. When a child experiences an event he knows that is happening, experience does not lie. Not only is the event true but the conclusions he is drawing about the event appear to be true also." As a child we see and experience situations, but our young minds have not matured enough to understand what might have been the reason behind a situation or circumstance. In the "healing of memories," Jesus wants to bring a different perception of the event, one that brings healing to the hurt and pain of the past.

That is what He did for me when He showed me my mother handing me to Him at my birth. My feelings of rejection were released, and I could look at my mother through new eyes. I could see her heart, the one He knew was there but I had not perceived or felt.

The little girl in me was still holding onto a lie. Jesus revealed the Truth. I could look past all my disappointments and begin to see my mother in a different light. My heart softened, and a flood of emotion washed over me. I could now reach past my pain and look at hers. My heart began to break for the pain and suffering, the disappointments, the brokenness that she had experienced in her life.

The interesting thing is that I could not be the person I am now if it had not been for what she had poured into my life. She was an overcomer, and she took adversity and made the best of it. She modeled that for me. Those times when she was missing from my day-to-day life were because she was making sacrifices for me. It could not have been easy for her to take on the financial responsibility for our family when my dad became ill and was fired from his job. I could count on her to take care of me. She was a generous, giving person, but all too often (in the eyes of that little girl), I felt she gave to everyone else, not me. Until I let go of some of the misconceptions that that little girl had, I couldn't grab hold of the beauty within her. That little girl inside of me needed to forgive her for the disappointments I felt because of the "lies" I believed.

Are you believing "lies" about your mom? It is worth considering. Maybe you don't believe they are lies. You may have been actually abandoned and so abused, so neglected that you can't see past your pain. How you were treated was wrong. You may not be able to see any good in your mom. But I know that if you make the decision to forgive your mother, you'll experience a freedom and a peace you may never have known. What was done to you may not have been right and your forgiving it does not let her off God's hook, but it does release you from the torment that you have carried. You are the one who suffers when you hold onto all that resentment, anger, bitterness, and hatred. Releasing her will be an avenue to your healing, and as unforgiveness leaves, you make room for God's love, peace and joy.

How do you think that would feel?

I want you to take a moment here and imagine your mother saying these words to you. They may be words you may never have heard or may never hear from her lips, but they may be words you have longed to hear. As you read you may grieve, you may weep, you may even scoff, thinking "Yeah, right!" But your Heavenly Father understands that void in your life. He also knows what you need to hear and what will bring you healing and freedom. Receive them from His knowing heart.

My daughter,

How I hurt you.
In so many ways I have hurt you.
Your heart was bleeding
And I didn't see it.
I was so selfish
So centered on my needs that I ignored yours.

What a gift you were to me
And I didn't take care of that gift.
So many times you cried out to me, but I didn't hear.
I was too busy or too hurt myself to pay attention.
All those times when you were saying,
"Look at me, Mommy. Did I do good?"
All you needed from me was an "Atta girl!"
You didn't get it.

You felt abandoned because you were abandoned—
If not physically, then emotionally.

As I think about that now
How it hurts my heart.
I was a failure at being a mom.
I let you down.

Now you have grown into womanhood,
But an empty place that should have been filled with my love
Is filled with resentment, anger, bitterness, and maybe even hatred,
Not only toward me, but perhaps toward others and more importantly
toward yourself.

You may have felt unworthy of love,
Because the one who was supposed to love you most kept it from you.

Yes, I know now the pain that I caused that little girl inside of you
And I am so sorry.
I know it's hard to forgive that kind of pain and it isn't even fair for me
to ask, but I will:
Will you forgive me?

Will you please forgive me for all the hurt and pain you suffered because
of me?

I was wrong.
You were a little girl needing a mommy to run to
Needing a mommy hug
Needing to hear the words, "I love you."

I can't take back the time, the years, the experiences.
I can only ask for your forgiveness
And pray that you will grant me that gift.

I don't deserve it—I guess that's why it has to be a gift.
Just like the gift that Jesus gave to you and to me,
The undeserved gift of forgiveness when He died on that Cross,

He suffered as He gave that forgiveness.

It will be hard for you, too.
Can you do that?
Will you do that?

I know that if you can and if you will, we will both be healed in the
broken places of our lives.
I can only ask.
I love you, my daughter.
I love you.

Mom

CHAPTER FIVE
Who Me?

But there is more to my story, my healing. This is a chapter I have hesitated to write because it not only exposes myself, but also addresses an area that is very controversial. I shared my doubts with a friend who works in prison ministry, and she said I needed to tell it. "If you don't, how will people get free?" People needed to know the truth.

As I thought about it some more, I became convicted of my need to share this part of my story because it has been a major part of healing in my life. My goal and I believe God's purpose in writing this book is to bring you to a new place of freedom and for you to find the healing in your life that He so desires for you. I have to tell it.

I don't know about you, but a lot of life can be spent trying to measure up to other's expectations. We want so much to be loved and accepted. We want to "make it" in someone's eyes. There seems to be a deep cry within us, "Doesn't anybody really care? Can't anyone love me just the way I am? What do I have to do to be loved?"

When that cry in our heart is not met, when we feel rejected, we put up walls to protect us from being hurt. Hurt can be at the root of resentment, anger, bitterness, hatred, and unforgiveness. We have been hurt so we want to hurt back. We may want to hide, or we may want to relieve the pain by running to alternative sources like alcohol, drugs, or sex. "How can I get rid of that pain? How can I get relief? How can I begin to break free from the bondage I am in?"

My people are destroyed for lack of knowledge.
(Hosea 4:6 NKJV)

There are so many things I did not know. I had a rude awakening.

I attended church most of my life, but no one told me that there is an enemy who has come "to steal, and to kill, and to destroy" (John 10:10 NKJV). But I found out!

I didn't know anything about Satan or his influence and power on the lives of people. My mother knew nothing about him either, so she could not prepare me for what was to come next.

I discovered that Satan is alive and well and has an army of spirits who do his bidding. Those spirits are everywhere, but Satan who is the "father of lies" doesn't want us to believe any of it. It's called deception.

I have also come to discover that God, too, has an army—an army of angels who are there to do God's bidding and to fight for His children.

I attended a conference not knowing what was going to happen, but believing it was something God wanted me to do. I asked my husband, who is a pastor, what he thought would happen at the conference. He said, "Well, you might see some demons leave." My reaction? "You've got to be kidding!" The only thing I had ever heard about demons was not good. I had memories of the movie, The Exorcist, and they were not good memories.

At the conference, prayer was offered for those who were looking for freedom from such things as rejection, self-hatred, pride, unforgiveness, anger, and others. My heart's desire was to be free from anything that might interfere with my relationship with God, so I went up for everything. As I stood waiting to be prayed for about the "spirit of anger," I couldn't help but think of different people I probably harbored some anger toward—my parents, my brother, my first husband, my abuser, and yes, I may have been holding onto some anger toward my present husband. It was my turn. As I stepped forward, the prayer minister placed one hand on my shoulder. With that, a growl and a scream came from somewhere inside of me! It lasted a few moments. When "it" stopped, I was in total shock, thinking, "This can't be happening to me!"

My husband was seated in the front row, and he, too, was in shock. Suddenly the "Word of God" became more real for him and for me than it had ever been. Demons are for real—and his wife had one!

His comment, "And I've been sleeping with that!" brought a laugh, but I wasn't laughing on the inside.

It took several weeks for me to comprehend what had happened that day. My immediate reaction was one of shock, embarrassment, and shame, but also an awakening. My eyes were opened to some things I had been blinded to all of my life. The Bible is true. What Jesus did on the cross set me free from a bondage I didn't know I had. There is a real enemy out there who comes to steal, kill, and destroy.

In John 10:10 (NIV), Jesus says, "*The thief comes only to steal and kill and destroy: I have come that they may have life, and have it to the full.*"

Have you ever wondered why you get locked into patterns of thinking and acting that are destructive? You beat up on yourself, and by your own efforts try to break free from some habit or behavior that you know isn't who or what you want to be. But you continue to fail.

People looked at me that day. Some said, "I can't imagine that you could have a 'spirit of anger.' You're always so nice. You don't act angry."

I had to ask myself the same question. When I did, I realized that I had "stuffed" my anger all my life, and it had become a stronghold on my life. It never occurred to me that in so doing I had opened the door for that "spirit of anger" to get a foothold in my life.

It was after that time that the Lord revealed, through my inner healing experience, the time and place where that spirit of anger (and abandonment) had gained a foothold in my life—that moment when I saw my mother and father leaving me to the lusts of a trusted friend. I had stuffed it, and "stuffing it" became a pattern for me—a habit and an opportunity for the enemy to gain access to me.

I had thought that the inner healing experience I shared earlier in regard to my sexual abuse was the end of my healing of that experience, but I was wrong. If this "inner healing" is for real, then I should be able to go to Jesus anytime and ask Him to reveal truth to me. So, I did just that.

In my quiet time one day, I asked Him to reveal the next place He wanted to bring healing. I sat and waited for some time when once again I saw Him. He was taking me back to the place I had been abused again. I thought I'd been healed of that! Why was He taking me there again? I didn't want to go back to that place (perhaps a clue that I needed to). Yes, I questioned Him.

He took me to the window of that garage apartment, put his arm around me and had me look out the window to see my parents driving away. I was angry and I felt abandoned. I felt the Lord revealed to me in that moment that that was the place where a spirit of anger and abandonment came into my life. My parents didn't know it because I never told them, but those feelings were real. A little six-year-old girl didn't know what to do with them. They were leaving me in a place of deep wounding, and a painful memory was seared into my spirit.

In those moments the painful feelings surfaced, but only for a moment. Then I saw Jesus lift me up on His shoulders and carry me to another room where He played with me, twirling me around. We giggled and laughed together. Joy returned to my heart and spirit. He was making a new memory, a happy one. I then saw Him take me by the hand and lead me through a set of doors. He closed the doors behind us. It was over. A hurtful, damaging memory had been healed by the love of Jesus. The feelings of abandonment were gone, and along with them the guilt, shame, and condemnation I had carried for so long.

Can you see what happened here? The spirit of anger left me at this conference, but it was only later as I prayed for inner healing that it was revealed to me how that spirit gained access to me. It wasn't until the Lord gave me a new understanding and perception of that situation that I was healed of the trauma, the wounding that had occurred. I needed to be healed of the hurt and pain that came with feeling abandoned by my mother. I was healed, and I was then able to forgive my mother.

Are there events or traumas in your past that may have opened the door for the enemy to gain a foothold in your life? Is there a moment in time when you saw your mother walk away from you, when you felt abandoned, physically or emotionally? Were there moments when you felt anger toward your mother, but never told her, never expressed it? There may be experiences that you have suppressed because they were too painful. Those are opportunities that the enemy uses to gain access to you. It is only as we bring them to the One who came to set us free that the lies are exposed and the truth revealed—that we find the freedom He so wants to give you.

Following that day, that experience, I have since come to know and understand that there are spirits in the supernatural realm waiting for an opportunity to oppress you in some way. In many ways it was a good revelation for me, because up until that time I would blame myself for some attitudes and behaviors that I had that I thought were a "bad me," never realizing that there can be spirits that would manipulate and control my thoughts. Have you ever done that?

There was another discovery I made through that experience that made the Bible true for me. It is only at the name of Jesus that demons flee. Does that verify what Jesus did, or not?

Many do not believe that a Christian can have a demon. I used to believe that until that moment in time when "the lie" became "truth" for me. I know that a Christian cannot be demon possessed, because you are possessed by the Holy Spirit. The spirit part of you is completely filled with the Holy Spirit, but there is a soul part of each of us that consists of the mind, the will, and the emotions. That is where the enemy attacks.

He can oppress us by attacking our mind first—our thoughts. What we think about and how we think about it will affect our emotions (our feelings), which in turn cause us to act in a certain way (our wills). That is the method of operation of Satan. He is called the "father of lies" because he lies! His biggest lie is that he doesn't exist. That was the lie I believed all of my life until I encountered the truth. It is a lie that a Christian can't have a demon. Another lie is that I could never have a demon. All of those lies, I believed.

Some will say that I must not be a Christian. If that is true then I don't know what a Christian is. I gave my life to Jesus forty years ago. I have been baptized in the Holy Spirit. From the moment I committed my life to Jesus, I have had a hunger in my spirit to pursue Him, to know Him. I have come to love Him enough to commit all that I am to Him. The Bible and His Word are my daily bread. I believe my life is bearing the fruits of the Spirit, and I believe those who know me would say they are "good fruits."

Having said all that, I have also come to discover that the primary way we open the door to Satan and his army of evil spirits is by holding onto unforgiveness. I didn't know how important that was. The anger that seethed below the surface of my consciousness wouldn't make room for forgiveness.

Countless times in the Bible we are told that we must forgive. In Matthew 6, we find the Lord's Prayer. We say it often, but do we think about what we are saying? In vs. 12 it says, "Forgive us our debts, as we also have forgiven our debtors." But if you will look just past that to verses 14 and 15, He says, "For if you forgive men when they sin against you, your heavenly Father will also forgive you. But if you do not forgive men their sins, your Father will not forgive your sins" (NIV). Whew! I want to be forgiven, don't you?

There are consequences to holding onto unforgiveness. I found that out, too!

In Matthew 18:32–35 (NKJV), Jesus tells the story of the unmerciful servant. There was a king who was willing to forgive his servant for a large debt, but the servant went out and instead of forgiving the small debt of a fellow servant, he had him sent to prison. When the king found out, he became angry and said,

> *"You wicked servant! I forgave all that debt because you begged me. Should you not also have had compassion on your fellow servant, just as I had pity on you?" And his master was angry, and delivered him to the torturers until he should pay all that was due to him. So [Jesus continued] my Heavenly Father also will do to you if each of you, from his heart does not forgive his brother his trespasses.*

What does that mean for those of us who refuse to forgive?

It means that we will experience consequences, and usually we are the ones who are tortured or tormented because we cling to resentment, anger, and bitterness. Most of the time the one we need to forgive isn't bothered. We are the ones who are suffering. We feel that resentment, that anger, that bitterness, and it affects our attitudes, our words, our responses, our actions. We have been hurt, so we hurt others. Then we hate ourselves. Feels like torment, doesn't it?

Who is the torturer, the tormentor? Satan. When we refuse to forgive, Satan has the right, the permission, to torment us.

When I first discovered the way that Satan operates and the fact that demons are everywhere just waiting for an opportunity to torment and manipulate us, I became preoccupied and started to use demons as an excuse for every bad thing in my life. It became a distraction for me. I started thinking about demons and Satan more than Jesus and His Word and His promises. What a mistake that was! They are not equals. Satan is a created being and under the feet of Jesus. Jesus is divine and has defeated the works of Satan by His sacrifice on the Cross. But, we need to be prepared. God's Word shows us how to prepare.

Be prepared. You're up against far more than you can handle on your own. Take all the help you can get, every weapon God has issued, so that when it's all over but the shouting you'll still be on your feet. Truth, righteousness, peace, faith, and salvation are more than words. Learn how to apply them. You'll need them throughout your life. God's Word is an indispensable weapon. In the same way, prayer is essential in this ongoing warfare. Pray hard and long. (Ephesians 6:13–18 TMSG)

I needed to learn how to apply His Word to my life. I heard a teaching one time by Scott Bauer,[5] Jack Hayford's son-in-law, who is now with the Lord (but his teaching lives on after him in my mind and heart). He talked about the movie *Apollo 13*. When the astronauts were trying to return to earth, all of the instruments they needed for direction were not reliable. There was one scene where Tom Hanks said, "If I can keep the Earth in the window, we can keep a straight course" (I'm not sure of the exact words so the paraphrasing is mine). Scott said that if we "keep Jesus in the window," we'll find the right direction.

When times have become rocky for me, I am reminded of that. I need to keep "Jesus in the window" of my life.

What I have come to discover is that the more time I spend at the feet of Jesus, reading His Word, listening for His voice, singing His praises, sharing "my stuff" with Him, the more I have come to love Him and the more I have felt His love.

I don't know how many of you have seen *The Wizard of Oz* or read it, but there is a place where water is poured over the "Wicked Witch" and the witch actually dissolves into a puddle! That's what I believe happens to Satan when God's love is poured into our lives and received by us. Satan's stronghold on our lives dissolves.

There is no fear in love. But perfect love drives out fear.
(1 John 4:18 NIV)

God's love is perfect.

We need to know that God's Word has provided the answers for victory over the enemy of our souls and that He is our ultimate protection when we are submissive to Him.

Submit yourselves, then, to God. Resist the devil, and he will flee from you.
Come near to God and he will come near to you.
(James 4:7,8 NIV)

Humble yourselves before the Lord, and he will lift you up.
(James 4:10 NIV)

We have wonderful assurance in Psalm 91 (NIV).

He who dwells in the shelter of the Most High
will rest in the shadow of the Almighty.
I will say of the Lord, "He is my refuge and my fortress,
my God, in whom I trust."
Surely he will save you from the fowler's snare
and from the deadly pestilence.
He will cover you with his feathers,
and under his wings you will find refuge;
his faithfulness will be your shield and rampart.

You will not fear the terror of night,
nor the arrow that flies by day,
nor the pestilence that stalks in the darkness,
nor the plague that destroys at midday.
A thousand may fall at your side,
ten thousand at your right hand,
but it will not come near you.
You will only observe with your eyes
and see the punishment of the wicked.

If you make the Most High your dwelling—
even the Lord, who is my refuge
then no harm will befall you,
no disaster will come near your tent.
For he will command his angels concerning you
to guard you in all your ways;
They will lift you up in their hands,
so that you will not strike your foot against a stone.
You will tread upon the lion and the cobra;
you will trample the great lion and the serpent.

"Because he loves me," says the Lord, "I will
rescue him;
I will protect him, for he acknowledges my name.
He will call upon me, and I will answer him;
I will be with him in trouble,
I will deliver him and honor him.
With long life will I satisfy him
and show him my salvation."

CHAPTER SIX
He Loves Me?

How could He love me? He doesn't know all the awful things I have done. He doesn't know the anger and hatred I have felt, the terrible words I have spoken to others, the crummy attitudes I have had. He doesn't know how much I have blamed Him for all the bad things in my life.

Yes, He does. He knows it all—and loves you just the same. He knows the guilt, shame and condemnation you have taken upon yourself. He knows that you have hated yourself even though He loves who you are. He offers you freedom and His unconditional (yes, unconditional) love.

Healing your relationship with your mother can never be fully realized until you come to know more fully God's love for you. Sometimes we expect too much from our mothers. There is a dimension of love that we long for that we may expect our mothers to fill, but can only be filled by God's love.

Very often the image we have of God comes from our impressions of the authority figures in our lives, usually picked up in early childhood and usually our parents. If we feel loved and accepted by our parents, we will probably perceive and easily understand God to be a loving God.

On the other hand if we were fearful of our parents or feel like we could never please them, we may project those experiences on God. So right here, healing needs to take place and a new perception of God and His great love for us needs to be conveyed.

We can look at Jesus and see the wonderful sacrifice of love He made for us to die on the cross, but what about Father God? Do you see the heavenly Father as an unrelenting judge; and Jesus as the One who loved us enough to die for us? But Jesus Himself says:

He who has seen Me has seen the Father.
(John 14:9 NKJV)

If you are a parent, perhaps you can understand the heart of God and the sacrifice and pain He must have felt to offer His son to pay the price for our sins. How His heart must have ached to see the pain and suffering of His Son.

The love of God has been poured out in our hearts
by the Holy Spirit who was given to us.
(Romans 5:5 NKJV, emphasis added)

God's love is poured out for us, but too often we don't comprehend or receive it because we don't feel worthy of being loved. That's a place where Jesus, through His Spirit, can reach deep down inside and bring healing. Listen to what Jesus says in His own words.

I have loved you even as the Father has loved me. Remain in my love.
(John 15:9 NLT)

There is no greater love than to lay down one's life for one's friends.
You are my friends.
(John 15:13, 14 NLT)

You are His friend. He laid down His life for you.

I am leaving you with a gift—peace of mind and heart. And the peace
I give is a gift the world cannot give. So don't be troubled or afraid.
(John 14:27 NLT)

Don't let your hearts be troubled. Trust in God, trust also in me.
(John 14:1 NLT)

My purpose is to give them a rich and satisfying life.
(John 10:10 NLT)

I have come as a light to shine in this dark world, so that all who
put their trust in me will no longer remain in the dark.
(John 12:46 NLT)

I have come to save the world and not to judge it.
(John 12:47 NLT)

Come to me all of you who are weary and carry heavy burdens and
I will give you rest.
(Matthew 11:28 NLT)

In His final words from the cross:

Father, forgive them, for they don't know what they are doing.
(Luke 23:34 NLT)

It sounds like love to me.

That kind of love is yours. He offers it to you—yes, to you. Are you beginning to feel it?

I was blessed to have a father who showed me tenderness, love, and care. I grew up feeling loved so it was easy for me to fall in love with Jesus. But I did have some fears regarding Father God, not just awe and respect, but fear of punishment if I didn't do everything just right.

My mother was the disciplinarian in my family and did not spare the rod. Perhaps that's where some of that fear came from. I was afraid not to please her. I thought I had to earn her love by being good. That, too, was a lie I believed until healing took place in my life and I knew that the discipline came out of her love and desire to do what was best for me.

Until I forgave her and received that love, I had a hard time breaking free from the legalistic trap of trying to earn "brownie points" in order to be loved by God. How about you?

What God wants most is for you to receive His love and for you to love Him. It is a love relationship He is looking for—He's not looking for you to be perfect. He wants you to come to Him, just the way you are, right where you are. He longs to hold you and love you into wholeness.

It's so easy to get caught in the trap of "I have to be cleaned up before I can come to God." That's where Jesus comes in. When He died on the cross, He took all "that stuff" upon Himself. With Jesus in our hearts, God looks on us as holy and blameless. Through Jesus, we can come to Him in all our brokenness and He will put the pieces back together.

It's not by our striving, but by His unconditional love that we are healed and restored. It's not by keeping "all the rules" that we are accepted and loved, it's a gift that we receive when we open our lives to receive Jesus. As we submit to Him in our weakness and acknowledge our "screw ups," our sins, and ask for forgiveness, forgiveness is given and we are a new creation in Him. He starts the restoration process. His Holy Spirit comes to live and abide in us and will guide and direct our lives.

The Lord says, "I will guide you along the best pathway for your life. I will advise you and watch over you."
(Psalm 32:8 NLT)

And you will find that the more you come to love Jesus and receive His love, the more you'll want to obey Him.

We love because He first loved us.
(1 John 4:19 NIV)

And may you have the power to understand, as all God's people should, how wide, how long, how high, and how deep his love is. May you experience the love of Christ, though it is too great to understand fully.
(Ephesians 3:18, 19 NLT)

One day as I was praying, I cried out to God, "Lord, I have come to know and to love you so much and have felt your love. It is so easy to tell these women that You love them, but how can I help them to really feel that You love them."

He gave me these words to give to you.

My Daughter,

I have such a longing for you to know Me and to trust Me with your life.
I see your every tear, I hear your every cry.
I understand when you shake your fist at Me and say, "Why, God, why?"
My heart grieves for the pain you have known—the heartache you have experienced.
I know that every little girl needs a mother and a father who love her just the way she is.
I know that your mother and father have made choices that have hurt you.
I want you to turn to Me.
My arms are open wide, waiting for you to come to Me.
I want to fill that hole in your heart.
I want to fill that place with My perfect love—
My perfect love that "casts our all your fears":
That fear of being abandoned.
That fear of never being good enough.
That fear of failure.
That fear of never being able to please those you love.
That fear of rejection.
I understand those fears as no one else can
I have been with you from the moment you were conceived.
I have seen every hurt, every broken place in your heart.
I came because My heart hurts so much for yours.
See Me holding your broken heart in My warm and tender hands, the warmth of My love being poured over it like oil, seeping into every crack and crevice, smoothing the wrinkles and healing, healing, healing.

Hear Me say, "I love you, _____ [insert your name].
I love you so much that yes, even today, I would die for you to show
how deep My love is for you."
Believe it!
Receive it.
> *Your Heavenly Father*
> *The perfect Father*

You have been searching for that kind of love all your life. His love is a gift, but a gift needs to be received. Receive His gift of love for you. Pick it up, embrace it, hold on to it—it is yours. Yes, yours forever and ever.

59

CHAPTER SEVEN
But How Can I Trust Him?

"**H**ow can I trust God?"

Is that a question you have asked?

"When I was crying out, 'Mommy, where are you?' God, where were You then? I've prayed, and You, God, haven't answered my prayers. How could You give me the mother/the father I have? What kind of loving God are You anyway? I don't feel loved, I feel condemned. If You can do anything, You could have changed things, made my life better. Why, God, why?"

How often there has been that cry in our hearts coming from the deep pain that has gripped our lives in some way—those cries of desperation. "If only I could believe that God loved and cared about me in those moments and that His heart hurt for me, I might be able to trust Him."

"Trust is the fruit of a relationship in which you know you are loved" (from *The Shack*[6]).

When I look back on my life and my relationship with my mother, yes, there were many disappointments. But as I have come to see my mother through His eyes, He has brought to my mind some special impressions about her that prepared me for rough days ahead. I recall my mother spending each morning in a quiet time talking to God. She didn't talk a lot about God to me, but she modeled a trust in Him that has stayed with me through the years. I didn't realize the influence that had on my life, until I was challenged by life's circumstances and had to lean on Him in ways I never had before. The seeds of trust had been planted, and through the wind, the rain, and the storms, those seeds took root and began to grow.

It takes time for trust to grow, and it grew in my life because of the storms. You don't need trust when you can handle life on your own. It's when you can't that the cry for help wells up within and you look to someone or something to lean on. Because of those seeds planted by my mom, I knew to whom I should run, the One to whom she had run , so many times in her life.

There have been many storms in my life. Some have felt like hurricanes with high winds and heavy rains that beat against those seedlings, but in the process, strengthened them.

Very often we don't realize what we've had until we have lost it or are about to lose it. That realization came to me when my mother was diagnosed with leukemia. My mom had leukemia! It was like a stab wound in my heart. Suddenly all of the disappointments of the past fell away, and I saw my mom through the eyes of love. I wanted so much to make her last days meaningful and beautiful. I watched the courage she had as she faced the everyday challenges. I saw her strength fail and the blush of her cheeks fade until that day when we said our goodbyes. My heart was broken. The mommy I would want to run to in the days ahead was gone. I had to run to Him, and He met me in my pain.

It says in His Word that "*He has sent Me to heal the brokenhearted … To comfort all who mourn*" (Isaiah 61:1,2 NKJV). He did. Memories of the good times flooded my mind and heart. I was able to move on to the next place my faith and trust would be tested.

Two months after my mother died, my dad died suddenly from a heart attack. I think he died of a broken heart. Following her death, I saw him give up on life. I wasn't with him when he died. It was sudden. I had no warning, no opportunity to say my goodbyes. How that hurt. Here was my dad who had loved me so tenderly during my life, and I didn't get a chance to say goodbye. Once again I was steeped in grief.

I didn't have my mom to run to. The void in my life was huge. I was an orphan now, but not in God's eyes. He had adopted me as one of His own, and once again, I ran to Him. His arms were open wide ready to hold me and comfort me, but it took time before that healing was complete. Even now, thirty years later, tears well up in my eyes as I remember walking to that graveside and seeing them laid to rest side by side. I walked away that day with two big holes in my heart that only He was able to heal.

Little did I know that I would be faced with some of the same emotions my mother had to deal with only two years later, when I was diagnosed with breast cancer. When I went into the operating room, the doctor was pretty certain that the lumps were benign, but unfortunately he was wrong.

For those of you who have experienced that, you know the feelings that accompany the loss of a breast or breasts to cancer. The diagnosis of cancer is bad enough, but when what you have felt is a dominant part of your femininity is gone, your identity is shaken. You begin to wonder, not only if you are going to live, but if you do, how is your life going to play out? I had been married just a year. My right breast was lopped off! I looked at myself in the mirror—no vestige of a breast. The right side of my chest was flat—totally flat. How would my husband respond? Would he still want me? What would be his thoughts, his reaction?

The thoughts of death loomed ahead of me. The doctor had given me a 50/50 chance of survival. Even though my husband was by my side, I felt so alone and knew that this would be a walk I would have to take by myself. How I would love to have had my mommy to run to. She would have known what I was feeling. She had walked this path. She wasn't there, but I remembered the courage she had in the face of death. With God's help, I summoned that courage. Hope and joy returned.

My husband loved me through that time, and through him I was feeling the unconditional love of Jesus. He was Jesus with skin on, especially in those moments when I was feeling ashamed of my bodily image or when I was throwing up because of the chemotherapy I received. I did have reconstructive surgery a year later, and I have to say I felt better about myself, but best of all, God healed my body of the cancer. It's been over twenty years now.

Six months after my cancer surgery, my husband was diagnosed with a serious melanoma. It was stage four, and his prognosis was as bad, if not worse, than mine. He had surgery and the melanoma was removed, but the thought of losing him to cancer loomed large. My questions: "Where are you, Mommy, now?" and "Why, God, why?" Fear gripped me. That old fear of being abandoned again dominated my thoughts and feelings.

A year before my mother died, I went through a divorce. That was not a part of the plan I had for my life. Those of you who have been through divorce know well the devastating effects it can have on your sense of self worth and value. I think that if I knew then what I know now about the designs of the enemy to steal, kill, and destroy, I would have been better equipped to fight the battle to save my marriage and save my children from the anguish, hurt, pain, and sorrow that my husband and I inflicted upon them. The hurt and pain that I experienced growing up does not compare to the hurt and pain that this mommy laid on her children. I'm sure that they could say, "Mommy, where were you? How could you let this happen? Don't you know that we love you both? We want and need you to be together."

Divorce wreaks havoc. When I think of how many lives were crushed and dreams destroyed, my heart grieves, even now, but I do know that God has forgiven me.

Many of the influences of childhood we carry throughout our adult lives. I am certain that some of the insecurities and fears I had, unknowingly, carried into my marriage. As a result, I failed in my marriage and I failed to protect my children from the very things that had been missing from my life—security and trust.

One by one the props of my security were being knocked out from under me. I had to lean on God. I leaned, and He held. I didn't fully realize His faithfulness until all the props were pulled out from under me.

I had wanted God to answer my prayers my way. When things became so bad, when I had screwed up royally, when life hit me hard in unexpected places, I gave it all to Him. I got out of His way, and then the puzzle pieces of my life began to fall into place.

Worth and value can be elusive. When we try to live up to others' expectations for our lives, we look for our worth and value in the eyes of others. I could not see any talents or special gifts in myself. I was constantly comparing myself to others and coming out on the short side. I was still trying to be okay in my mother's eyes. I wanted to earn her love by doing something exceptional. I didn't see the gifts and abilities that God had given until He revealed them to me.

I began to see that it was through my life's struggles and hardships that He was developing the gifts that He wanted to use to fulfill His purposes for my life. Too often we are so busy doing "our thing" that we don't recognize the fact that that isn't His thing for us. Once we discover His thing, how easily our lives begin to flow in the river of His life and love. When His plans and purposes for our lives are fulfilled, we finally feel fulfilled.

I have heard people liken life to a beautiful tapestry. It is beautiful on one side, but knots and strings are going every which way on the backside. It's the backside that helps create the beautiful side. It took time and perspective before I saw the way God has used my life experiences, the knots and strings, to weave a tapestry that is gradually forming into something beautiful and of value. But, there was a large segment of that tapestry yet to be woven.

Those seedlings of trust were growing stronger and stronger, but a test of their strength came about in a most unexpected way. Another storm was coming over the horizon.

It was Friday, May 11, 1990. It was my birthday, and my husband Vern had planned to take my side of the family out to lunch to celebrate. (This was a second marriage for both of us, so we had his-and-hers kids.) We had come to town to participate in his daughter's wedding, which was to be held that Saturday. We were waiting on all my children to gather at my daughter's house before we went out to lunch, when the doorbell rang.

A man in a suit was at the door and asked Vern to step outside. We didn't know who he was until he stepped back inside with my husband whose face had drained white. All I could say was, "What's wrong?" The man was an FBI agent who had come to arrest my husband on orders from the prosecutor in Charleston, South Carolina.

He proceeded to question my husband and all of us as to why we were in New Jersey. When my daughter showed him the wedding invitation, he was a little embarrassed, but undaunted. He told us he needed to take my husband to Newark to go before a judge there.

Meanwhile I looked out the window. There were four other FBI agents surrounding the house. We were all in shock! I can only imagine what my three-year-old granddaughter was thinking and feeling as she looked on. My husband said that he was thirsty. Obviously the adrenalin had kicked in, but he had to be escorted to the kitchen to get a drink of water by two FBI agents. We had not had lunch. It was getting past lunch time, but suddenly no one was hungry.

The next thing we knew, they were escorting him out the door and into a car. I had to know where they were taking him and after some questioning they told me.

All of a sudden our lives were turned upside down.

As it turned out, unknown to us, the day before, an indictment had come down against my husband. The prosecutor in South Carolina had thought he had "skipped town" and was a "fugitive from justice," so had called in the FBI to find him. I don't recall how they figured out where we were.

Once the FBI agent in charge discovered why we were there, he became more compassionate, but said that unless they could find a judge willing to hear his case on a Friday afternoon, my husband would probably be in jail for the weekend.

How I cried out to God, "Help, Lord, help!"

I needed my mommy! This was all beyond my comprehension or understanding. I don't remember when exactly in the scheme of things that I turned to the Bible, but when I did, I opened to a verse that became a lifeline to me in the days, weeks, months, and years ahead.

> *Trust in the Lord with all your heart*
> *And lean not on your own understanding;*
> *In all your ways acknowledge Him,*
> *and He shall direct your paths.*
> *(Proverbs 3:5 NKJV)*

That was only the beginning of seven long, difficult years, but when we were able to reflect back, we could see God's hand at work in it all.

Early in our marriage we had made some good investments in real estate and prospered. After we both had cancer, we moved to Hilton Head, South Carolina. While there, Vern did counseling and I went back to nursing school.

We made some investments with some of our assets, in a gold mining operation in Nevada. After my husband had gone to Nevada with a friend and my son to check out the proposition, we felt it was a credible operation. We invested, and many of our family members also invested.

Because of our enthusiasm for the project, when another project was started, my husband was asked to help sell it. He would receive a commission much as a real estate or an insurance agent might receive. Unfortunately the government concluded it was a fraud and shut down the operation. Vern was accused, along with twelve others, of fraud and conspiracy. The twelve others pleaded guilty and received a small fine and a short probationary period. Because we knew that Vern had believed in the project and was not guilty, we decided to go to trial.

We went through the first trial. It was going well for us when the judge declared a mistrial because the prosecution failed to come up with some evidence that was required. We felt that that in itself was a victory and we thought it would all be over, but the prosecutor decided other-wise and decided to take us to trial again. We were told by one friend who was asked to join the prosecution that the prosecutor had gathered all his witnesses together. They were coached so that their testimonies would be in alignment.

Our witnesses were still the same and the prosecutor knew exactly what their testimony would be, so in the second trial we did not fare well. The jury was out, and it was growing dark in the courtroom as we waited for the verdict. How I wish I had my mom sitting next to me.

I did not know it, but at the same time I was in one room praying, my husband was praying in another. We were both praying the same prayer: "Not my will, but Thy will be done, Lord."

Of course we expected that His will would be that my husband would be found "not guilty." God knew He was not guilty, I knew he was not guilty. The verdict had to be "not guilty"! The jury returned. I can recall there was such a heaviness in that courtroom that it could be felt. Their verdict: "Guilty!"

We were all in shock as you may well imagine. How could this be? What does all this mean? Where do we go from here? Was this indeed God's will? So many questions.

It was about this time when once more I was crying out to God saying, "Why, God, why?"

He spoke to me again in His Word. It was one of those times when I opened my Bible and the Lord reached out to me through these verses:

"For I know the plans I have for you," declares the Lord, "plans to prosper you and not to harm you, plans to give you hope and a future. Then you will call upon me and come and pray to me, and I will listen to you. You will seek me and find me when you seek me with all your heart."
(Jeremiah 29:11–14 NIV)

This was the hope I needed for our future at a time when I felt despair and hopelessness. I felt God was reaching out, wrapping His arms around me, and taking me to a new place of trust in Him.

The days, months and years ahead were filled with many trials. I don't mean courtroom trials, but God amazed us by His faithfulness. Vern could have been sentenced to from two to five years in prison. Instead, the judge said he had been awakened at four a.m. the day of the sentencing convinced that Vern was the least culpable of all the defendants. He decided that he was going to deviate from the government guidelines and sentenced Vern to two months house arrest and four months in a halfway house. The judge said he would be allowed out to work and believe it or not, to teach Sunday School.

Those times when I was alone at night, how I would have loved having my mom to talk to or to just be with me. Perhaps you have had times like that when you were going through a difficult time and just wanted your mom to be there for you.

We lost our home in Hilton Head and we felt we would probably never own a home again. I had had some assets from my first marriage, but all of my husband's were tied up. We thought that perhaps if we could find a house with an assumable mortgage, we just might be able to purchase a home again. One of our daughters came to visit. As she and her father drove around, they found a house that we thought had an assumable mortgage, but when we went to the bank we found it did not. The banker asked me how my credit was. I told him that it had been good up until a few months before, but that it probably wasn't that good now. He then asked me what my income was like. I told him I wasn't making much money. He said those are the things the bank examiners would be looking at. I told him, "Yes, I know. It would take a miracle for you to give us a mortgage!" His reply, "Well, I believe in miracles!" A little surprising coming from a bank lender wouldn't you say? We left there not knowing what the outcome would be.

The bank gave me a mortgage!

Unfortunately Vern had to go through bankruptcy. All of our assets were depleted, but time after time the Lord met our needs in unexpected ways. People would drive up to our house and tell us that the Lord had told them to give us five hundred dollars. We received a check in the mail from my brother right before the electric and phone were to be shut off. We received another check in the mail given to us by one who said the conditions of the check were that we would tell no one where it came from and we were to do the same for someone else when we could. That came just in time to pay our mortgage. People stopped by the house with bags of groceries and on and on and on. How can you not trust God when those kinds of things are happening time and time again?

Have you ever had someone reach out to you in kindness un-expectedly? Did someone step in when your mom let you down? Have you ever had a situation or a circumstance that seemed bleak at the time, but ultimately something good came from it? You were left on your own feeling abandoned, but in the process grew stronger and learned how to discover gifts and abilities you never knew you had. Could that be God reaching out to you through someone or through a circumstance? These can be trust builders. They were for me.

We had our low moments—some extremely low. I can remember the time when Vern sat on the couch, tears streaming down his face. I heard him say,

"I don't see how God can ever use me again in the ministry I have been called to."

He had received a letter from the conference he belonged to saying he "was never to teach or preach in the name of Jesus again." I could feel his broken heart. But we were reminded again that God heals broken hearts.

He came home one day and told me how he felt like such a failure and a poor provider. He had returned from the food store. He had had $5 in his pocket, and as he returned to the car with some milk and perhaps a few bananas, he wept again. Some of all that had happened to him was catching up to him.

But God is full of surprises, and there were many out ahead of us. In Psalm 37:4 (NKJV) it says,

Delight yourself also in the Lord, And He shall give you the desires of your heart.

That never became more real to me than the time when Neil Diamond was coming to Charleston. I have always loved Neil Diamond. The thought crossed my mind that it would be great to see him, but there was no way that could happen so I kept those thoughts to myself. I knew Vern would have loved to take me, but he, too, knew it was not possible with our financial situation the way it was.

We worked all day and decided to go to Ryan's (a local inexpensive buffet) for supper. When we walked in the door, there was a man standing next to the cashier. He said to us, "Would you like two tickets to go to see Neil Diamond?" You could have knocked us over! He then went on to say, "You'll need to eat dinner here because we don't want them to lose the business, so you may be a bit late."

We ate quickly and headed to the Coliseum. When we arrived there the concert had already started, but as we walked in another man met us and said, "May I see your tickets? There's been a bit of a mix up, and these are your tickets." The seats were in the front row! I believe that for the first time in my life I had actually seen angels. I felt that was a very special gift from God at a time when we needed a boost to our spirits. He knew the desire of our hearts—and we had not said a word.

When we had first moved to Charleston we attended a couple of different churches over the period of a few years and found love and support in each one, but it seemed God was moving us in a different direction. One Sunday we attended a church out of curiosity. We had driven by it daily. We were so moved by the sense of the presence of God in that place that we never stopped attending.

The first Sunday following church, a young doctor and his wife invited us to a small group in their home. It turned out we were with a number of young couples who quickly embraced their "seniors." We stayed with that group until such time as we felt the Lord wanted us to start a group in our home. For the first time in many years, Vern started to feel like God was using his gifts again.

Our group grew, and we involved ourselves in several other activities in our church. It was wonderful to be used by God again, but He had another big surprise for us. Vern was asked to come on the staff of Seacoast Church, the church we had been attending.

Sometime after Vern came on staff, he was asked to preach at one of our Wednesday night services. After the service I approached our senior pastor, Greg Surratt. I said, "Greg, it took a lot of courage for you to put Vern on staff. Thank you." His response, "I've done worse things. Besides we wouldn't be a New Testament Church if we didn't have someone on staff who had been in prison!"

We both laughed, but that evening was such a mountaintop experience for Vern and me. We had been in the valley for a long time—seven years—and God was restoring and redeeming one of His precious sons.

That was only the beginning of the restoration process. For the past twelve years, God has used Vern and me in ways we could never have imagined and in ways that would not have been possible if we had not gone through the valley to discover the faithfulness of our Heavenly Father. We have learned to trust Him in a way we would never have known had we not had to depend on Him in the darkest days of our lives. He has been faithful through it all and has revealed the plan He had for us. His plans were to prosper us and not to harm us, to give us a hope and a future. I knew He loved me.

We felt like we had been sent to death row, that it was all over for us.
As it turned out, it was the best thing that could have happened. Instead of
trusting in our own strength or wits to get out of it, we were forced to
trust God totally ...
And he did it, rescued us from certain doom. And he'll do it again, rescuing
us as many times as we need rescuing ...
Now that the worst is over, we're pleased we can report that we've come out
of this with conscience and faith intact, and can face the world—and even
more face you with our heads held high. But it wasn't by any fancy footwork
on our part. It was God who kept us focused on him,
uncompromised.
(2 Cor. 8–10, 12 TMSG)

The seeds of trust that were planted early in my life unknowingly by my mother grew and became strong through the battering of the winds and rain of the circumstances of my life. My trust in God has become deep rooted. Although the answers to my prayers have not come packaged in the ways I have expected or wanted, He has been faithful and has turned adversity into the plans He had for my life—my future. The "tree" of trust has grown strong and has prepared me for the rest of my life.

God doesn't waste pain. He won't waste yours. You may not see where He is taking you, but if you keep your eyes on Him, He will bring good out of your pain, heartache, suffering, and sorrows. You just may be the seed that He plants in the life of another to bring hope to a hurting heart.

Trust Him.

CHAPTER EIGHT
Help!

Help! Where do I go from here?

I have been hurt. I have been abandoned. I have been mad at God. I have blamed God. I have been angry and resentful. I have held onto bitterness and resentment. I have refused to forgive. There were times when I have held hatred in my heart toward someone. How could they do that to me? God, how could You let them do that to me? Don't You care?

Yes, My child, I do care—very much.

I have been held in the grips of self-pity, self-hatred, guilt, shame, condemnation, lust, pride, fear. There were generational influences of the occult in my life, but He has delivered me out of them all and continues to deliver me when they raise their ugly heads again.

It has been a long uphill journey. But with each step, I have drawn closer to the One who called me by name. The journey has been upward from darkness to light, from the pit to the mountaintop. There were moments when I felt the exhilaration of a freedom from my past and I felt the Lord moving me to a new place, a place from where it had been "all about me" to becoming a vessel He could use to reach out to others. I then discovered joys I had never known before.

The first thing you need to ask is, "Do you want to get well?"

That is the question that Jesus asked a man who had been an invalid for thirty-eight years.

"Sir," the invalid replied, "I have no one to help me into the pool when the water is stirred. While I am trying to get in, someone else goes down ahead of me."
(John 5:6 NIV)

He made excuses and blamed others for not receiving his healing.

Do you like living the way you're living? Do you like the way you are feeling? Or do you want to see a change in your life, a change in your attitudes, and in your relationship with your mother and others? Do you want to get well?

I have shared what God has done in my life. He has healed me. He has changed me from the inside out, and He offers that to you.

Once you decide, "Yes, I want to be healed, I don't want to spend the rest of my life carrying all this baggage," you have taken a giant step toward becoming the person God created you to be, with the freedom, peace, and joy He offers.

He is the One who can bring about that healing, but you need to ask Him. He is the "Helper." He doesn't force Himself on anyone. You have the choice to accept or reject the love He offers. It is love, an unconditional love, the kind you may never have known or experienced. When you ask Him to come into your life and ask Him to forgive your sins, He will. He will begin the transformation from the inside out.

Once you have done that, follow these steps.

Look to "His Word," the Bible, as your instruction manual.

If you have never read the Bible, find a Bible that is easy for you to understand. There are several recent translations that are good and are written in modern day language. I have used the New King James Version, the New International Version and the New Living Translation. The Message is easy to understand, but is a paraphrase and not a translation.

When you get a Bible it is easy to think you need to begin at the beginning, but I would recommend beginning with the Gospels in the New Testament. The Gospel I suggest reading first would be the Gospel of John. It is like a love letter from God.

After reading the Gospels, I would suggest that you continue in the New Testament through the book of Acts and into the letters that follow. Then move to the Old Testament beginning with the Psalms and

Proverbs. By then you will be comfortable with the Word and can head to the beginning with Genesis.

The Old Testament lays the foundation for the New Testament and the coming of the Messiah, Jesus Christ.

As you read you will begin to sense God speaking to you through His Word. Sometimes it will actually quicken your spirit. It is a word meant just for you. The more you read and study His Word, the more you will come to know God, who He is, how much He loves you and the plans He has for your life.

This Book can be your guidebook for living, if you will let it.

Confess your sins.

In the book of James, it says, "*Therefore confess your sins to each other and pray for each other so that you may be healed*" (James 5:16 NIV).

It wasn't easy confessing "my secrets" to anyone, but the relief and freedom I felt as a result convinced me that it was essential. I don't recommend confessing sins to just anyone or to everyone. You need to find someone you can trust. If you don't find that in a person, God loves it when we come to Him and are totally honest and transparent with Him. I think that is one of the greatest compliments you can give another, that you trust them enough to risk exposure and judgment. The beauty of confessing to God is that He doesn't condemn you. He does convict you, giving you that nudge that prompts you to want to confess, but He does not condemn you.

So now there is no condemnation for those who belong to Christ Jesus.
And because you belong to him, the power of the life-giving Spirit
has freed you from the power of sin that leads to death.
(Romans 8:1,2 NLT)

He is glad when you are willing to acknowledge your sin, your failures, your mistakes, and He is ready to forgive them and to bring healing and restoration to those broken places in your life. He wants to know you that well and for you to know Him. That's called intimacy. Does it ever feel good to know and to be known by someone and loved just the same.

I remember reading a book one time by John Powell, *Why Am I Afraid to Tell You Who I Am?*[7] The premise of the book is, "I am afraid to tell you who I am because I'm afraid you won't like me." I know I have had that fear. Have you? But what I have discovered is that with God, there needs to be no fear. He wants you and loves you just the way you are. As you draw into a closer relationship with Him, He will do the perfecting of your life. You don't have to be good and certainly not perfect or without sin to come to Him. He just wants you to come. Yes, He wants you to be sorry for your sins and to go and sin no more, but it is by your desire and His power that it is even possible.

I don't know how many times I have tried to be "good," tried to change by my own will and power, only to fail time and time again. But I have found that as I come to Him, confess my failures and ask for His help, which comes through the power of His Holy Spirit, I have been able to walk away from temptations and attitudes that were destructive. How often was that cry of "help" in a moment of weakness. He heard, and He responded.

Jesus said,

> *And I will pray the Father, and He will give you another Helper, that He may abide with you forever—the Spirit of truth, whom the world cannot receive, because it neither sees Him nor knows Him, but you know Him for He dwells with you and will be in you.*
> *(John 14:16, 17 NKJV)*

The Holy Spirit is called the "Helper," and He helped.

Forgive those who have hurt you.

> *Be kind and compassionate to one another, forgiving each other, just as in Christ God forgave you.*
> *(Ephesians 4:32 NIV)*

Unforgiveness seems to be the biggest obstacle to being healed, whether it be emotional or physical.

You need to forgive your mother. You may need to forgive God. He doesn't need our forgiveness of Him, but we need to let go of the bitterness, anger, and resentment we hold onto because of the times we prayed and He didn't answer our prayers the way we thought they should be answered or He didn't meet our expectations in some way and we were disappointed in Him. You may need to forgive yourself. Sometimes that is the most difficult. "What do I need to forgive myself for?" Only you can answer that question.

You say, "I could never forgive my mother. You don't know what she has done to me. You don't know the abuse I experienced through her words, her actions. She abandoned me! How can I forgive that? She didn't care about me, she just cared about herself. I'm supposed to forgive that? She wouldn't believe me when I told her I was being sexually abused by my father, my brother, my stepfather, my uncle. She left me when I needed her. She died! Why did she die? Doesn't God know I needed her? What kind of God is He anyway?"

Does any of that stir up feelings in you?

Forgiveness is not a feeling. You probably don't feel like forgiving. Forgiveness is a choice, a decision, one that God wants us to make. As we read about forgiveness in His Word, it is not a request by God, it is a command of God. He would not command us to do something we are unable to do. He wants us to make the decision to forgive and then He will help with the feelings.

You may say, the hurt is too deep. "I can't even bring myself to say 'I forgive.'" When you forgive, you are not saying that what someone did to you was right. What was done to you may have been very wrong, but we have a God who is a just God. He knows the situations and circumstances surrounding your pain, and He doesn't let the perpetrator off the hook.

Yet he does not leave the guilty unpunished.
(Exodus 34:7 NIV)

Let Him be your vindicator if you find it difficult to say "I forgive
_____." Talk to your Heavenly Father and say, "I release _____ to
you. I trust You to make things right." Release them, and along with
your decision the resentment, anger, bitterness, and hatred will begin to
dissolve. You'll experience a freedom you may never have known before.
The enemy has lost his right to torment you.

This is probably the most difficult step for you in finding the
freedom and healing you seek, but it is absolutely the most essential.
Trust the one who has forgiven you for so much. You will not be
disappointed. The heaviness you have carried for so long will be lifted
from your heart and given to the one who said,

*"Come to me, all you who are weary and burdened, and I will give you rest.
Take my yoke upon you and learn from me, for I am gentle and humble
in heart, and you will find rest for your souls. For my yoke is easy and
my burden is light." (Matthew 11:28–30 NIV)*

"Rest for your souls"—doesn't that sound wonderful? It is
wonderful!

Spend time with Him sitting in His presence.

Be still before the Lord and wait patiently for him.
(Psalm 37:7 NIV)

Delight yourself in the Lord and he will give you the desires of your heart.
(Psalm 37:4 NIV)

You will seek me and find me when you seek me with all your heart.
(Jeremiah 29:13 NIV)

Be still and know that I am God.
(Psalm 46:10 NIV)

Have a conversation. You don't have to know a fancy prayer. All He wants you to do is to share from your heart and be honest with your feelings. It's okay to express your frustrations with Him. Then, take time to listen.

Ask Him to reveal the places in your life that He wants to heal, then just wait. He may bring a thought or a memory to mind that you have no memory of, but He does. His Word says:

Jesus Christ is the same yesterday and today and forever.
(Hebrews13:8 NIV)

God has said, "Never will I leave you; never will I forsake you."
(Hebrews13:5 NIV)

Even though you may not know Him, He has known you all your life, yes, even before you were born. He is the one who:

... knit you together in your mother's womb.
(Psalm 139:13, paraphrase mine)

Ask Him to reveal Himself to you in a way that you will know and understand and to heal you in that broken place in your life. The reason He came was:

... to heal the brokenhearted,
to proclaim liberty to the captives,
and the opening of the prison to those who are bound.
(Isaiah 61:1 NKJV)

Let Him. I don't know how He will reveal Himself to you, but He knows the best way.

Write to Him.

Something I have done that has been especially meaningful for me is to get a notebook and write to Him, pouring out my sorrow, anger, frustrations, disappointments, but also to thank Him for what He has done in my life and to help me "remember" those times when I cried out to Him and He did something amazing in my life. It helps to look back, especially in those times of new challenges, to be reminded of His faithfulness. I am also learning to wait when I get finished saying what I want to say to see if He has anything to say to me. All too often I rush off to do "stuff." I have found that if I wait, He will surprise me, guide me, or simply give me some words of encouragement.

Be still, and let Him lavish His love on you.

My favorite times, now, are those times when I'll put on some soft music and just sit in His presence, allowing Him to pour out His love on me and returning my love to Him in words or in song. I have no words to describe the healing and peace He has brought to my relationship with my mother and to my life, but my prayer is that you, too, can and will:

… grasp how wide and long and high and deep is the love of Christ,
(Ephesians 3:18 NIV).

I'll take the hand of those who don't know the way,
who can't see where they're going.
I'll be a personal guide to them,
directing them through unknown country.
I'll be right there to show them what roads to take,
make sure they don't fall into the ditch.
These are the things I'll be doing for them—
Sticking with them, not leaving them for a minute.
(Isaiah 42:16 TMSG)

Praise the Lord, O my soul,
and forget not all his
benefits—
who forgives all your sins
and heals all your diseases,
who redeems your life from the pit
and crowns you with love and compassion,
who satisfies your desires
with good things
so that your youth is
renewed like the eagle's.
The Lord works
righteousness
and justice for all the
oppressed.
(Psalm 103:2–6 NIV)

And that means you …

CHAPTER NINE
Cinderella
(A Modern Parable)

I don't know if any little girl has not heard, read, or watched the story of Cinderella. Have you ever felt like Cinderella?

Would you believe that God knows that story, too? He knows how many little girls have that secret wish to be loved and rescued from the hurt, pain, abuse, abandonment to have the perfect prince come and carry her away from it all and take her to a new life.

It was 2:00 a.m. I couldn't sleep. I was tossing and turning, needing guidance for the next session of the "Where Were You, Mommy?" class. I went into our "Son Room," a room my husband and I retreat to, to spend time with the Lord. I kept hearing the word "Cinderella." *Cinderella? Why am I hearing that? What does it mean?*

I heard, "It's a parable! It's a parable that a little girl will understand."

I don't often hear a word that clearly; it was almost audible.

"What am I supposed to do with that?"

I started to reflect on the characters in Disney's version of the story of Cinderella and all the pieces fell into place. I began to understand what He wanted to say to that little girl in you. He wants to bring encouragement and hope to you. He wants to show you a picture of His love for you. He wants to show you that He understands.

Cinderella would be you, the little girl who felt abandoned, unloved. Her mother had died or was not there for her. She had a deep longing for someone to fill that hole in her heart. She had a deep longing to be loved and accepted just the way she was, by someone. Is that the way you feel?

The Stepmother is the mother or authority figure who neglected or abused her. Is there someone in your life that fits that description?

The Stepsisters are those people in her life who put her down in some way, by words or actions, or were jealous of her. Anyone you can think of?

Lucifer, the cat is who else but the enemy who came to kill, steal and destroy her life. She didn't know about him either, but she recognized the evil in him and felt its effects on her life.

Gus Gus, and all the other mice, birds, etc., came in the form of God's precious creatures to bring her hope and help. The family of God (God's human creatures filled with God's love) can bring hope and help to your life, if you will open the doors and windows of your heart to receive.

Bruno, the dog, one of God's angels (like Michael), came to her rescue! God has sent angels to help you.

Isn't it obvious that all angels are sent to help out with those lined up to receive salvation? (Hebrews 1:14 TMSG).

That would be you when you accept what Jesus did for you.

The Fairy Godmother is the Holy Spirit who came to give her the gifts she needed to fulfill the purposes God had for her. He can and will do that for you.

The Prince is Jesus, who searched the whole kingdom until He found her and won her heart.
He is searching for you and will keep on searching for you until He finally wins your heart.

The Glass Slipper is the perfect fit for her foot and hers alone. God has a perfect plan for your life that is a perfect fit for you. It isn't like the one He has for others, so you don't ever need to be envious or jealous of others. He wants you to flow in the stream of the gifts and strengths He has given you and the life He has planned for you, so that you will know and experience the fulfillment you so long for.

The King is our Father God (who wants offspring!). It was the king's dream that there would be grandchildren that he could love and adore. God's desire is that as you come to experience His love, His forgiveness, His healing, as you abide in Him, you, too, will bear much fruit.

"I am the vine, you are the branches. He who abides in Me, and I in him, bears much fruit; for without Me you can do nothing" (John 15:5 NKJV).

As this cast of characters unfolded I became more and more excited because it all fit together, something only God could have done in a way that would speak to a little girl's heart.

Jesus taught His followers by telling stories—parables. This one is specially designed by Him for the little girl in you.

"With many stories like these, he presented his message to them, fitting the stories to their experience and maturity. He was never without a story when he spoke. When he was alone with his disciples, he went over everything, sorting out the tangles, untying the knots"
(Mark 4:33, 34 TMSG).

Here is a story of a young girl. Her mother has died. Her father dies and leaves her to be cared for by a stepmother who abuses her. Her stepsisters poke fun at her. She works hard trying to please everyone around her. Her dream is that one day a prince would come who would love her just the way she is and would give her a new life filled with joy, peace, and his undying love, who would love her enough to die for her. Some love, huh?

Enter, Jesus, your Prince.

All your life He has been pursuing you, hoping one day you will open the door and let Him in. You open the door, and you look into the eyes of love. His arms are open wide, waiting for you to run to His embrace. He loves you so much. He wants you so much. He wants to take away all your pain, all your sorrow. He brings with Him gifts for you—gifts of love, joy, peace, compassion, understanding, healing, forgiveness. Yes, He is even willing to die for you—He loves you that much. His heart cries out to you.

"Come to me, run to me—I'm waiting. You are My Princess!"

The Lord prompted me to show Disney's animated version of Cinderella to the "Mommy" group. They saw that story through different eyes as I told them the cast of characters the Lord had revealed to me. May I suggest that you visit or revisit that film. You may be surprised at the reaction you have to it as you see it as God's desire to bring hope to that disappointed little girl locked inside of you.

At the conclusion of the "Mommy" class, a crown was placed on the head of each of these women – a crown made especially for them.

Jesus came to do that for you. He is your Prince. Because you are His bride, you are His princess and the daughter of a King. He loves you as if there were no one else to love. The glass slipper is designed to fit only you, the unique, one-of-a-kind person you were created to be. The crown is to remind you of who you are "in Him".

You did not come from your parents, you came through your parents. Before you were conceived, God had the perfect you in mind. You were His creation.

Think about the moment you were born. Picture Jesus holding you and saying, "Isn't she beautiful? She's just what I wanted." Then He hands "baby you" to the "adult you." Can you say to the "baby you," "You are beautiful and I love you"? Try it. Yes, that little girl inside of you needs to hear you say, "I love you, and I'm so glad you were born."

God wants you to love yourself, and it starts right at the beginning. We love because He first loved us. Yes, your Prince was willing to die for you to prove His love for you. Believe it, receive it.

God wants you to know who you are "in Him" (Eph. 1:5–13 NIV). In Him you are chosen, adopted, accepted, redeemed, forgiven, an heir, predestined according to the purpose of Him who works all things according to the counsel of His will. Having believed, you were sealed with the Holy Spirit.

God wants the little girl in you to know that in His eyes you are precious, honored, and loved (Isaiah 43:4 NIV). He will never leave you or forsake you (Joshua 1:5 NIV). You are His daughter, and His love for you is unconditional and permanent. You are His princess and His bride.

Take a moment now. Sit in a quiet, comfortable place and let these words from a Father who loves you, seep into your heart.

My Child,

The words you have read are words
I wanted you to read
But more than that,
The healing that occurred in Migsie's life
I want to bring to your life.

She has spoken My truth into your life.
Yes, before you were born, I knew you.
I planned your life.
I have the perfect plan for your life.

Many have made choices to try to thwart the plans I have for you.
Yes, there is an evil one who prowls around
Seeking those he wants to destroy.
If I didn't have a purpose for your life, he wouldn't care.
But he is under My feet, and he is under yours.

As long as you keep your eyes on me
And walk with me through the days of your life,
I will never leave you or forsake you. That is My promise.

You are precious to Me, My child.
I want only the best for you.

There will continue to be challenges in your life,
But every challenge you face and press through
You will become stronger.
And I will use your newfound strengths
To bring hope and victory into the lives of others.

But for now just know
How very much I love you
How precious you are to Me

I didn't create you for pain and sorrow
I created you for joy
And a life filled with the assurance
That you are Mine

> *My daughter*
> *My princess*
> *My bride*

My love isn't just for now, but for eternity.
Step into the life I prepared for you.
I'll walk beside you every step of the way.
Trust Me.

Lean on Me, child, lean on Me
I love you for now and for always.

Your Heavenly Father

> *For you have a new life.*
> *It was not passed on to you from your parents*
> *For the life they gave you will fade away*
> *This new one will last forever*
> *For it comes from Christ.*
> *(1 Peter 1:23 TLB)*

My Prayer

Dear Lord,

You know so well the hearts and hurts of these women. You know every struggle they have had. I pray, Lord, that the veil will fall from their eyes and they will see, maybe for the first time, Your face, that they will feel Your love. If it were not for Your love for me, this book would never have been written. You have peeled away, layer by layer, the bruises of my life. I lay them open for all to see because I know the freedom that comes from the Truth. Your Word says, "The Truth will set you free," and it has set me free.

I know that there are many who are afraid to take that first step. There has been so much wounding in their lives that they feel they can trust no one. You know it wasn't easy for me to take that first step. I had to be in the bottom of the pit looking up before I reached for Your Hand, which brought me up and out of the darkness into the light.

This journey has been a long one with many joys and many sorrows, but it has been through the struggles and failures of my life that I have come to know that I can depend on You. You have loved me through it all even when I was at my worst—and there have been a lot of "worsts"!

You have known my deepest, darkest secrets. Through Your patience and Your long-suffering, You have moment by moment, step by step, led me to higher ground. I feel that "higher ground" is rock solid under my feet now.

Lord, I have so much gratitude in my heart for the way you have transformed my life. I pray that the women who read this book will truly come to know Your love, which is so wide, so deep, so kind, so gentle, so patient, so forgiving, so healing, that the hole that has been in their hearts will be filled to overflowing and they will experience a transformation in their lives. Lord, I know you have a plan for their lives, but without the healing You want so much to bring, Your purposes for their lives will be blocked.

Lord, open their eyes to see and their hearts to receive all that you have for them.

Thank you, Lord. Thank you.

So hear, dear one—and receive. Take what you need, discard what you don't need , but hold onto the One who wants to bring out the "perfect you" that He planted the moment you were created. He loves you so.

My Love, Migsie

References

1.   David A. Seamands, *Healing for Damaged Emotions* (Colorado Springs: Chariot Victor, 1991)

2.   Norma Dearing, "Teaching: Addictions and Inner Healing," St. Michael's Episcopal Church, Charleston, SC, July 27, 2005

3.   William P. Young, *The Shack* (Newbury Park, CA: Windblown Media, 2007), 154

4.   Mary Pytches, *Dying to Change* (England: new wine international, 2001), 16

5.   Scott Bauer, *Jesus Christ the Deliverer—Keeping Him First* (Van Nuys, CA: Glory Communications Intl., 1999)

6.   William P. Young, *The Shack* (Newbury Park, CA: Windblown Media,2007), 126

7.   John Powell, S.J., *Why Am I Afraid to Tell You Who I Am?* (Allen, TX: Resources for Christian Living, 1998)

About the Author

Migsie Jensen is the wife of Vern Jensen, an associate pastor at Seacoast Church in Mt. Pleasant, South Carolina. Together they have seven children and spouses and twenty grandchildren—and one great grandchild.

Migsie is a retired registered nurse. Since her retirement, she has been fully engaged in working alongside her husband in various areas of ministry in the church.

She has led small groups and has been asked to speak on numerous occasions in different venues. She is presently co-leading a small group with her husband and is actively involved in the prayer ministry of the church.

Her passion continues to be for the healing and restoration of broken lives of women and for conveying God's love whenever and wherever He leads.

She was led to initiate the formation of a group called, "Where Were You, Mommy?" For several years, she has ministered to women who had not experienced a nurturing and fulfilling relationship with their moms. This group became the impetus to writing this book in the hope that many more women would be reached with the healing love of God.

TO CONTACT MIGSIE
or for information regarding select audio recordings and artwork:

email address: **mommwwy@gmail.com**

website – **mommywherewereyou.com**

Notes